A DIRECTORY
OF
ANTIQUE
FRENCH
FURNITURE

Books by F. Lewis Hinckley

A Directory of Antique Furniture
Directory of the Historic Cabinet Woods

A DIRECTORY OF ANTIQUE FRENCH FURNITURE

1735-1800

Over 300 Illustrations of Provincial, Parisian and Other European Antique Furniture

F. LEWIS HINCKLEY

CROWN PUBLISHERS, INC., NEW YORK

ACKNOWLEDGMENTS

I am grateful to Monsieur Gaston Bensimon, of Paris and New York City, for his time and interest in examining and commenting upon most of the photographs represented here, and for his valued opinions offered so graciously throughout the years.

Photographs specially taken in Europe for this project have been obtained through the cooperation of officials connected with the Musée des Arts décoratifs, Paris; the Musée Nissim de Camondo, Paris; the Musée Lyonnais des Arts décoratifs; the Musée Historique de Lyon; the Musée et Bibliothèque Calvet d'Avignon; and the Musée Historique Bernois. Additional courtesies in selecting reproductions were extended by the Archives Centrales Iconographiques d'Art National—Laboratoire Central des Musées de Belgique, Brussels—acknowledged by the accepted abbreviation "ACL Bruxelles" beneath illustrations made possible by their wide coverage of national treasures, also by the Musea Van Oudheden, Antwerp; the Musée du Château de Rohan, Strasbourg; the Musée d'Archéologie de Marseille; the Musée de Bordeaux; the Rohsska Konstslöjdmuseet, Göteborg; and the Rijksmuseum, Amsterdam. A number of photographs have also been provided by Monsieur Bensimon, and French & Company, Inc., of New York City, by Jacques & Henri Barroux, Paris, and by private collectors in Europe and America. Those photographs taken for me in this country, and others of pieces sold through the former American Art Association or through Parke-Bernet Galleries, Inc., were supplied by Messrs. Taylor & Dull, New York City.

Finally, I am grateful to my wife, Anne, for her appreciable contribution to this work.

Library of Congress Catalog Card Number: 67-24767
Printed in the United States of America

PREFACE

Furniture of the old French provinces is considered here under two principal categories, that which originated in Paris, and that produced in other major cities or towns. Attention is focused mainly on eighteenth-century designs introduced prior to the legal abolishment of these provinces, when France was divided and subdivided into departments, *arrondissements,* cantons, and communes. Considerations of eighteenth-century designs have been affected to some extent by misunderstandings in relation to Parisian furniture and to other French furniture which in general quality may be equal to or finer than much of that executed in Paris, but which, nevertheless, is frequently referred to as *provincial.*

French provincial furniture is a term that has been adopted in the vocabulary of the decorative arts, but which is frequently employed where other forms of phraseology would be more relevant and precise. In its application to the generality of collectible French furniture this term is either redundant or wanting in definitive significance.

Of the old French administrative districts or provinces into which the country was sectioned prior to the Revolution of 1789–1799, many contained one or more important cities in which thriving manufactories produced furniture of fair, medium, and excellent quality. Additionally, in the province of Île de France, wherein lay the capital city of Paris, and in various other provinces there were suburban localities in which members of the royalty maintained residences, and where they were at times supplied with specially made furniture of superior quality to complement other pieces obtained in Paris.

Provincial French furniture may be used in reference to pieces of a rural character, and which therefore lack sophistication or cosmopolitanism and refinement or polish. However, there are exaggerated beliefs, fostered at times by biased opinions, to the effect that all French furniture distinguished by the better qualities originated in Paris, and that pieces displaying surface treatments which deviate from those actually or supposedly representing Parisian work are *provincial.* Similarly, furniture produced by the Gillows in Lancaster, by the Seymours in Boston, or by David Roentgen in the residential town of Neuwied—for French, Russian, and German royalty—would also be *provincial.*

Furniture produced by master joiners and cabinetmakers of important French cities, other than Paris, was often fashioned after Parisian designs as well as with greater attention to specially developed decorative treatments. Local guilds saw to it that high standards of quality were maintained. Some artisans of these cities, and of smaller towns, received their training in Paris or in furniture centres larger than those in which they finally established themselves. Many acquired the benefits of techniques that foreign craftsmen introduced in the capital and elsewhere. In addition to designs and decorative treatments frequently varying from those favored in Paris, structural methods, which in general are less determinative of locale, were often superior to those employed by many Parisian masters.

French furniture that is truly *provincial,* which is therefore countrified and usually quite rude in appearance and workmanship, is given less attention among the illustrations in the *Directory,* as examples of this type are seldom worthy of reproduction. Such furniture was made by rural carpenters or joiners, or by others untrained in these trades, for use in modestly or humbly furnished living quarters, or in kitchens and pantries. Thousands of these pieces, produced during the second half of the eighteenth century or much later, together with mere fragments of others, have been rebuilt and refurbished to attract the eye of home furnishers with self-imposed flairs for the "old and quaint." With more selection and caution, often with little difference in outlay, this type of collector may acquire examples of Parisian or other metropolitan *menuisier's* (joiner's) work worthy of offer without quiet mention of "restorations," and which possess genuine charm in their undisturbed designs and soft-toned surfaces.

Some French authorities have inadvertently added to current misunderstandings of the more elaborate Parisian and other metropolitan furniture by illustrating such examples side by side, more often than not without any suggestions of provenance except those indicated by the locations of collections in which they appear, or formerly appeared. On the other hand, published illustrations of solidly constructed commodes and armoires, for example, produced by joiners of Paris and other French or Flemish cities, are frequently regarded as *provincial* from their sturdy character or supposed resemblance to the rusticity of country-made pieces.

In addition to this heavier work a more delicate but comparatively simple type of furniture was produced in Paris to supply the need and satisfy the taste of the average well-to-do citizen. Examples of this sort are frequently acquired as examples of *French provincial furniture.* Unknowing acceptances of such work as *provincial,* although executed by Parisian *menuisiers,* and occasionally by the most renowned Parisian *ébénistes* (cabinetmakers), are at times influenced by the fact that they may appear in various fruitwoods or other native timbers as well as in mahogany and the rarer exotics.

In the section of illustrations devoted to metropolitan furniture produced outside of Paris, all of the examples are offered as representing work executed in leading cities of the original French provinces; important centres associated with the manufacture of furniture for local use or export. As a result of the great interchange of technical skills that took place during the eighteenth century it is often difficult or impossible to specify the more cosmopolitan work of these cities and centres, at least with any degree of certainty, while in other instances it may be unwise to make definite ascriptions according to the limited amount of documentation available at present. Where some of the examples in this section and in the two sections that follow are wanting in the polish or sophistication to be found in a large proportion of French furniture, the choice of whether or not they may in this respect be regarded as *provincial* will vary according to individual interpretations of design.

The appended register of master *menuisiers* and *ébénistes* working in French provinces other than Île de France has been compiled and amplified as far as possible from the works of former authorities, more recently published findings, and through heretofore unrecorded marks that have been personally observed on French furniture of non-Parisian origin.

The vocabulary of terms applied to French furniture serves also as a means of condensing explanations and comparisons which otherwise would increase the size of the text and be more difficult to locate for reference purposes. Certain words and phrases are peculiar to the subject and are therefore not defined in French dictionaries or the usual works on antique furniture. (Many of the explanations are traceable to labeled drawings of eighteenth-century designers, whose names are given here where interpretations other than those originally intended may be, or have been, inferred.)

CONTENTS

DESIGNERS AND CRAFTSMEN OF PARIS AND OTHER METROPOLITAN FURNITURE CENTRES OF FRANCE

To appreciate old French furniture it is important that studies in this field be based in part on the historical and sociological backgrounds that are so amply covered in many works devoted to the subject. In order to acquire a more complete understanding of French furniture it is imperative that such studies be directed toward various influences affecting style developments and working conditions throughout the provinces into which the country was formerly divided.*

As France became the greater sphere of cultural activities during the sixteenth and seventeenth centuries, Italy was forsaken by many of her leading designers and craftsmen who emigrated principally to neighboring French provinces and to Île de France. Similarly skilled craftsmen were also attracted from the Netherlands and the German states. These migratory movements increased during the eighteenth century until there was a very large foreign population among the designers, cabinetmakers, marquetry workers, and wood carvers then employed in the leading cities and towns of France. In Paris, this influx of talent was increasd by visiting apprentices and journeymen from as distantly removed areas as Scandinavia, Austria, and Russia, traveling there to augment their training by study and work in ateliers of established designers and renowned artisans.

Prior to the eighteenth century dual influences emanating from Italy and the Netherlands were frequently merged in projects so modified by French conservatism as to become purely Gallic in their final interpretations. The same predominance of native forces is apparent in furniture produced during the eighteenth century, although there are numerous, often highly interesting departures from the norm.

This conservatism on the part of native French artists and craftsmen in their renditions of foreign themes has been summarized by Seymour de Ricci:

> The creative genius of the French artists has at all times dominated the influences to which it has been exposed. The atmosphere of strong corporate discipline, the force of an instruction and training received in common, as well as the poise and

* See under *Provinces* in the Vocabulary.

> moderation of the national taste, have always guarded the French craftsman both against a servile imitation of foreign works as also against an extreme exaggeration of their own characteristics. A man like Lebrun understood how to draw deep inspiration from the Italian baroque without falling into the excess of a Borromini; and even Bernini kept within the bounds of moderation the moment he began work for the French court.

Nevertheless, furniture executed by foreign-born *ébénistes, menuisiers,* and *sculpteurs en bois* after migrating to Paris, and to other important commercial centres of France, was at times quite exaggerated according to native tenets of design, as were the marquetry decorations supplied French *ébénistes* by *émigré marqueteurs.* In contrast the work of certain naturalized masters such as Oeben, Riesener, Beneman, and Weisweiler fell entirely "within the bounds of moderation" once they were established in Paris and actively catering to the tastes that existed there.

Of the artists who influenced early eighteenth-century designs produced in furniture centres distantly removed from Paris, J. Bernard Toro (1672–1731) of Toulon was responsible for introducing projects incorporating *mascarons,* dragons, and other chimerical effects that were favored in Aix, Arles, and other principal cities of southern France. Whether or not this particular influence reached from these localities to Paris, remarkably similar themes were later featured in the work of Cressent (1685–1768) and Nicolas Pineau (1684–1754), both of whom continued to promote *le Style Régence* far into the Louis XV period. (Pineau was one of the group of masters and artisans in various *métiers* who worked in Russia for some years under the patronage of Peter the Great and the Czarina.)

Just-Aurèle Meissonnier (1695–1750), an Italian from Turin, was one of the leading exponents of the later Baroque, or so-called Régence style, and of early Rococo projects carried out in France. He exerted a strong influence on the work of architects, joiners, carvers, and metalists during his period of activity. Of the elaborate designs which Meissonnier offered to a Parisian following, many came within the bounds of moderation, but those intended for translation in Portugal, Poland, or elsewhere in Europe were quite devoid of restraint.

In addition to his influence on Parisian work, Meissonnier's designs of circa 1735—such as those of a *fauteuil* and *siège* for the Baroness de Besvenal and a *canapé* for the Count de Bielanski—were apparently used some twenty-five years later in making certain of the plates Thomas Chippendale offered in London as *inventor* and *delineator* in his *Gentleman and Cabinet-Maker's Director.* (Indebtedness to Italian designers is more generally acknowledged in connection with earlier English furniture, but even Robert Adam owed much of his success to an Italian architect, Giuseppe Monochi, as well as to numerous lesser artists and mechanics of the same extraction.)

Although the majority of French artists and craftsmen were of native parentage some of the most prominent were sons of recent *émigrés,* their work being strongly affected by parental training and the usual propensities derived through ancestral transmission. It may be assumed that a certain proportion of the furniture produced in provinces other than Île de France would originate under these auspices. The most notable Parisian *ébéniste* of such a parentage was André-Charles Boulle (1642–1732), whose earlier projects in marquetry of metal or ebony and tortoise shell aroused not only the interest of his contemporaries but were repeated toward the close of the century by Étienne Levasseur (1721–1798), Philippe-Claude Montigny (1734–1800), and Georges Jacob (1739–1814).

The brothers Slodtz, sons of a Flemish sculptor "with more than a dash of Italian blood," are to be numbered among the designers instrumental in continuing the Baroque style long after the close of the Régence period. Following the death of Meissonnier, in 1750, Antoine-Sebastien Slodtz (1694–1754) was appointed *dessinateur de la chambre et cabinet du Roi,* a post later transferred to his brother, Paul-Ambroise, and then to René-Michel (Michael-Ange) Slodtz. The first two, who came to be known as *les frères Slodtz,* had been responsible for designing a commode executed in 1738 by the *ébéniste* Antoine Gadreau, and the metalist Jacques Caffiéri, for Louis XV's apartment at Versailles. They also supplied designs for the King's ornate *médaillier,* now in the Bibliothèque Nationale, and his more reserved *bibliothèque basse,* the drawing of which is preserved in the *Cabinet des Estampes* of the same institution.

Jean-Henri Riesener (1734–1806), a Westphalian by birth, added two cupboard sections to the latter production in 1784, and at that time also made a copy of the original piece—by no means an unusual procedure, for earlier designs continued to arouse Parisian interest during the closing years of Louis XV's reign and in the succeeding period of Classicism. Indeed, the drawings proffered by André-Jacques Roubo in *L'Art du Menuisier en Meubles,* Paris, 1772, included representations of examples dating from the *Siège de Dagobert en 630,* and through the Gothic, Renaissance, and Baroque periods, in addition to the usual Louis XV designs and others in the pure Classic taste.

Of the native French designers whose work retained some features of the Baroque style during the middle years of the century, Jean-François Blondell (1705–1770) is perhaps the most outstanding. Blondell was appointed architect to Louis XV in 1755, three years after the publication of his *L'Architecture-Français,* a work started by Daniel Marot (c. 1650–c. 1712), a designer connected with the atelier of Boulle prior to the revocation of the Edict of Nantes (1685) and his subsequent patronage by the Prince of Orange. Certain of Blondell's furniture projects feature *mascarons,* demi-figures, and a use of straight lines interrupted by Baroque scrolls—elements strongly reminiscent of techniques favored by Marot.

The Rococo, in its culmination as a highly sophisticated decorative style, is in truth a purely French development. This style has been authoritatively defined as "characterized by curved spatial forms, light and fantastic curved lines, often flowing, reversed, or unsymmetrical, and ornament of pierced shellwork . . . carried to extremes in Italy and Germany." Nevertheless, the French were the only interpreters of the Rococo movement who consistently adhered, in Parisian work, to sophisticated designs of light curved lines and elegant forms.

During the time that this vogue held sway in the French capital decorative compositions of southern Europe, central and northern Germany, the Netherlands, and Scandinavia retained a considerable degree of native restraint, or when elaborately curved lines or contours were featured these often lacked the subtlety and grace and the diverting artificiality of French treatments. In fact, Baroque designs or elements of such designs were continued and appeared predominantly in much of the work performed outside of France during the Rococo period.

While certain French artists retained Baroque themes or at least some formulas of the earlier movement during the middle years of the century, others attained a full development of the Rococo spirit as early as 1730–1735. That this supremely imaginative style continued to remain fashionable in Paris until circa 1770–1775 is attested in part by the designs published at that time by Jean-Charles Delafosse (1734–1789) illustrating seat furniture and cabinetwork in the full Rococo taste, along with examples following purely Classic lines.

Elements of this later Classicism had been proffered about a decade before the appearance in 1768 of Jean-François de Neufforge's *Recueil d'Architecture.* This publication, devoted partially to seat furniture, commodes, and buffets in the Classic taste, and the succeeding projects of such artists as Jean-François Boucher (1736–1781), provided solid foundations for the severe forms that were gradually introduced before and during the opening years of Louis XVI's reign. Ensuing Directoire designs were in many instances merely simplified versions of these forms, while various motifs that are more typical of this latest of the eighteenth-century decorative movements, such as the fasces, tambour, six-pointed star, quivered arrows, grouped banners, and other material trophies, had in fact been popularized beteween 1785 and 1790.

Joiners, or artisans, whose work was accomplished in solid woods, known in France during the eighteenth century as *menuisiers,* might produce only seat furniture and bedsteads; or tables, stands, commodes, and other case pieces; while the more versatile might turn their hands to supplying any or all of these requirements. Predecessors of the *menuisiers* were the *huchiers* or *huchiers-menuisiers,* and the carpenters or *charpentiers-huchiers* of earlier times who worked under statutes established in Paris during the fourteenth century, and in Rouen, Bordeaux, and other towns during the later years of the Gothic and Renaissance periods. When a *menuisier* was also qualified as a maker of fine veneered cabinetwork, or as a wood-carver, turner, or machinist, he was known as a *menuisier-ébéniste,* a *menuisier-sculpteur, menuisier-tourneur,* or *menuisier-machiniste.*

Ébénistes were highly trained cabinetmakers adept in the art of veneering and in the construction of basic forms embodying solid or built-up cores of oak, pine, or other common timbers, which they surfaced with finer woods. An *ébéniste* who was also an accomplished artist in marquetry work (and many were not skilled in this respect) was known as an *ébéniste-marqueteur.*

Menuisiers, ébénistes, and other members of the woodworking crafts, which included looking-glass makers (*miroitiers*) and turners (*tourneurs*), were banded together as members of local guilds existing in Grenoble, Bordeaux, Nantes, Strasbourg, Tours, Nancy, Metz, and various other leading cities or towns, including Paris. Each of these guilds elected from among its members a *jurande* or council of wardens *(jurés),* and a *principal* or *syndic* with an official rank similar to that of the agents or *syndics* associated with almost all of the ancient trading companies in Paris and other French cities. Guilds located outside of Île de France maintained long-established systems of apprenticement in which a candidate for acceptance as a master craftsman served his time under a master before he was permitted to submit a *chef-d'œuvre* or *pièce de maîtrise* for the approval of a council of jurors belonging to the guild in which entrance was sought.

The ancient society of *Maîtres Jurez Huchiers Menuisiers de Paris,* governed by sixty-two statutes and ordinances dating from 1580, was dissolved in 1743 and replaced by a new society operating under ninety-seven statutes, privileges, arrangements, and rules that were registered with the French parliament of 1751. In the new society, *La Communauté des Maîtres Menuisiers et Ébénistes de la Ville, Faubourgs, et Banlieu de Paris* (The Community of Master Joiners and Cabinetmakers of the City, Suburbs, and Municipal Areas of Paris), it was accepted that masters were free to follow any or all branches of work associated with joinery and cabinetmaking, although the majority specialized either in *menuiserie* or *ébénisterie.*

According to the articles of this new society elections of officials were to be held each year, within eight days of the celebration accorded its patron, Saint Anne. At these times a new *principal* or *syndic* and three jurors were to be elected by an assembly composed of the incumbent principal, six jurors, all former *syndics* and *jurés* remaining in the society, and twenty-four masters in good standing. The newly elected *syndic* could officiate for a year only, and should he die during his term of office the jurors and seniors would elect another member to his place, enjoined to serve for the balance of the term or forfeit any later attainment of that position.

No master could be elected as a juror unless fully qualified in his deportment and working skills, and not until he had been a master for at least ten years. Jurors officiated for a period of two years, and two brothers, or a father and son, were not permitted to serve as jurors or as principal and juror during the same period of time. It was the duty of jurors to see that unaccepted craftsmen *(faux ouvriers)* did not work in private houses or "even in convents, schools," and so forth, "and so deceive the public by the defective material and inferior quality of their work which they sell nevertheless in the name of the Community." They were also to watch those who bought work produced by interlopers and to seize such work whenever possible, aided if necessary by "the usher of the court, a constable, or even their guardsmen who will be at their disposition day and night." Confiscations were to be turned over "to guardians who will judge them, either to their defective wood or misshape . . . and in case there should be no sign of defective work no temporary repeal will be made except they be seen and tested by experts . . . to state the defective parts of misshapes." The jurors were permitted to keep half of the confiscated property, the other half going to the Community; and shortly after the yearly elections such goods were auctioned off at the office of the Community.

Jurors were to "visit four times each year all the masters and widows of the mentioned profession" who owned shops or workrooms in Paris or its environs, "also those who work on architectural wood structures, furniture, carriages, cabinetwork and veneering work, be it in oak, walnut, beech, elm, pine, ebony or other woods, and those who have storehouses and resell the works of the mentioned profession, without being obliged to ask any permission." For each of these visits a fee of ten *sous* was paid, half going to the Community and half to the jurors.

An applicant for admission in the Paris society continued to work under a master for at least three years following the completion of his initial apprenticement. He was then required to present proof of his full apprenticeship, a satisfactory certificate from the principal master he had served "for six years," and also, if he had changed his allegiance, one from the master or masters with whom he had worked since registering at the Community office. He was further judged on the basis of his masterpiece or *chef-d'œuvre,* and finally (with certain exceptions, *see below*) admitted to membership on payment of three hundred and fifty *livres* plus additional fees for various rights and taxes as stipulated in a declaration of 1691.

The applicant appeared before two assemblies, one in which he was presented and received his orders regarding the masterpiece to be produced, the other when his completed masterpiece was shown. These assemblies usually consisted of the *syndic* and *jurés* in charge, but they were larger if the applicant was the son or son-in-law of a master, a craftsman who had married the widow of a master, or was a stranger to the Community.

A son or son-in-law of a master who had attained the rank of *juré* or a craftsman who married the widow of such a master paid only one hundred *livres* to the Community after the acceptance of his masterpiece, plus additional fees for various rights and gifts. If the master in question had not attained the status of a *juré* the amount paid to the Community was one hundred and fifty *livres.*

Those who were neither sons, sons-in-law, or husbands of widows of masters, and those who were strangers, could attain their master's degree only after serving as associates of masters for at least six years counting from the day they registered at the Community office. They were then required to produce a certificate from a master, to make a more important masterpiece than usual in regard to size and quality, and to pay fifteen hundred *livres* plus the additional fees of other apprentices.

Widows of masters were permitted to continue the shops formerly operated by their husbands, either through the aid of a son or an expert associate or servant trained in the necessary skills. If the son of a deceased master or master's widow was not an accepted member of the Community he was granted three months to complete any work that had been started, and, if he desired, to attain a mastership in the Community. Should he not become a master by the close of this period and still continue to work for himself, all of his woods, tools, and equipment were to be confiscated and a fine levied upon him.

In keeping with long established rules concerning the execution of a masterpiece this was to be made according to prescribed "design, composition, contour, form and profile, quality and strength of wood." The work was to be carried out only in the house where the applicant was employed, entirely without assistance, and under the close inspection of a juror. Should an unaccepted craftsman pose as a master, even while making his *chef-d'œuvre,* he was subject to a fine of fifty *livres* and confiscation of his work, tools, and material.

Craftsmen working under any form of patronage, royal or otherwise, and who might thus "pretend to be masters," were enjoined to produce a masterpiece according to the established rules but under the inspection of a juror in his own workshop.

The rank of master was granted only to those belonging to the Catholic Church, apostolic or Roman, and of French birth or "in possession of a naturalization paper issued, verified and registered by" the Community.

A master *menuisier* or *ébéniste* could own but one shop or workroom in Paris or its environs, and he was obliged to reside in the district and house where his shop was located. He could, however, own a warehouse in another building and district, where he might work if the warehouse was not situated in a privileged section and if the door was kept closed so that none could see or know that such work was being carried on.

To insure the proper construction of all types of joinery, "be it of oak, walnut, beech, cherry or other wood," such furniture was to be produced "with great art," while any carving was to be carefully executed so as not to weaken any parts subject to stress and strain. Should it be discovered that a frame of any description had been weakened by an excessive depth of carving the carver was to be held accountable to the *menuisier* or the purchaser. Enrichments of all types were permitted, though, in contrast to accepted procedure in Italy and Germany, "sculptors, painters, architects and others" were not to be employed as collaborators under penalty of fines, damages, costs, and interests.

Chairs, tables, commodes, and other case pieces, including those for clocks, also frames for mirrors, paintings, or prints, "and all other work in cherry, walnut, oak, pine, beech, pear, olive, cedar, amaranth, ebony, palisander, violet wood and others not veneered," were to be carefully assembled with the use of tenons and mortices, wood pegs, and other necessary facilities for insuring the best possible craftsmanship. Pieces that were veneered with cherry, olive, ebony, violet wood, amaranth, palisander, satiné (*la Chine!*), or other *bois de marqueterie*, or that were enhanced with various metals, tortoise shell, mother-of-pearl, and so on, were to be constructed and finished with equal fidelity. Failure to meet these requirements was punishable by a fine of one hundred *livres*.

Every master was required to possess a special stamp for marking his work, the impression of which was to be registered on a sheet of lead kept at the office of the Community. In anticipation of certain craftsmen imitating the mark of more popular masters it was stipulated that a misdemeanor of this sort be punishable by prosecution and a fine of one hundred *livres*. It was further ordered that no master lend his stamp to another, or use it on the production of a "false worker." Those engaged as merchants in the furniture trade were not permitted to handle any new pieces unless these bore the maker's individual *pontil* mark, and only such pieces as a master was "forced to sell in order to live." Failure to observe this rule was punishable by a fine and confiscation of the illegally acquired property.

In addition to the individual *pontils* or stamps owned by joiners and cabinetmakers, the office of the Community kept a special *poinçon*, or punch, to mark all pieces that its members delivered over to the *merchands de meubles*. On ascertaining that such a piece had been properly signed by one of its members an authorized official struck the Community's mark immediately beside that of the marker. This mark consisted of the letters *J M E* joined together in the monogram **JME** , standing for *Jurande*—or *Jurés-Menuisiers-Ébénistes*. Nevertheless it has been misinterpreted by some experts as a shop mark standing for *"Maître Ébéniste"*—even in connection with honestly made and stamped seat furniture produced by *menuisiers* who confined their efforts to this other sphere of activity.

While it may be that officers of the Paris Community stamped a large part of the furniture requiring their particular attention, it is apparent that many of the working members did not pay strict attention to identifying productions which were unlikely to receive official inspection. This is indicated by the great number of unsigned pieces of outstanding quality that appear in French and other European collections of long standing. It is also obvious from the fact that in 1776 it was necessary to renew the order that furniture be properly stamped.

A *menuisier* or *ébéniste* working under royal patronage, and therefore permitted to use two *fleurs-de-lis* or the legend *Privilégié du Roi* in his mark, might be more attentive to advertising his status to a Parisian following—if such minutiae were ever of interest outside trade circles. This form of patronage was by no means confined to the environs of the capital, but was extended to masters of *Communautés* located in other cities of France, as in the case of Abraham-Nicholas Couleru, of Montbéliard, and Jean-Baptiste Topino, of Marseille.

Productions of masters working in such cities as Lyon, Marseille, Dijon, Grenoble, Nîmes, and Montbéliard are at times distinguished by their *pontil* marks, by holograph inscriptions, or, in the instance of a *marqueteur*, by an inscription made with a graver. However, furniture produced outside of Paris is more often unsigned—except of course those many pieces, of both fine and mediocre quality, that have been fraudulently supplied with marks in the names of prominent Parisian *menuisiers* and *ébénistes*.

During recent times it has become common practice with French *truqueurs* or other fakers to stamp unsigned furniture of Paris and other French cities, or of different European origins, with facsimiles of *pontil* marks employed by the most famous Parisian masters. Hence numerous fictitious "signatures" appear on genuinely antique examples as well as on reconstructed pieces, sometimes where unknown names have been removed, or even where original marks have been overlooked. More or less accurately rendered stamps have been supplied for this purpose, copied from original signatures or from published reproductions of such marks. The more resourceful forgers have been able to acquire original eighteenth-century *pontils* that have come into the market. Others have resorted to alphabetical punches, such as those retained by present-day craftsmen for honest purposes, but the singly stamped letters are seldom lined up with the precision of those made by a complete die.

To strike an impression on the seasoned rough or secondary wood of an article of furniture is the least troublesome task of a dishonest workman, or of a faker with no ability at all as a skilled mechanic. Hence, in catering to those whose collecting interests are centered on acquiring impressive signatures, there is little likelihood of detection in such an act—unless the style and working methods of the master whose name has been so used are recognized as differing from those appearing in a piece selected for this form of commendation, or unless there is some noticeable variation between the fraudulently impressed mark and that of the known purported maker's mark.

From the numerous examples of seat furniture which have turned up at auction during the past decades, produced but unsigned by French *menuisiers* and *maître menuisiers,* and which have been stamped with the names of *maître ébénistes* (*sic*), along with the **ME** mark, it is apparent that the decidedly varying skills of the *menuisier* and the *ébéniste* have to a very large extent been overlooked or otherwise disregarded by dishonest dealers, and by auction experts who have catalogued such spuriously marked pieces for public sale.

The practice became increasingly widespread as it was seen how gullible these experts and auction bidders had become; and as the masterworks of certain *ébénistes* increased in vogue, their names, along with ME stamps, were thus made to add materially to the prices asked and received for various pieces of furniture in either category of craftsmanship, extending even to out-and-out mediocrities, and sometimes to pure fabrications. In thus imposing upon the uninformed and misinformed, the French language has been disregarded to an extent where the term properly employed only with respect to the cabinetmaker has also been caused to include the separate, varying skills of the joiner. The present-day production of dies to produce these *pontil* marks and ME stamps has therefore increased with a corresponding disregard to names properly associated with makers of seat furniture, and with the MM mark denoting acceptances into their separate guilds as *maître menuisiers.*

In appraising or in formerly cataloguing old French furniture I have found it wise never to accord undue importance to any *pontil* signature, or to accept it as valid without proof of a substantial nature. Quality of design and craftsmanship, along with condition, should always be of far greater importance, and also the study of identifying characteristics, and comparisons indicating whether or not these are truly representative of a particular Parisian or other metropolitan *ébéniste* or *menuisier.* The collector, or expert, who is overly impressed by *pontil* marks is most easily duped, or likely to add to the wealth of misinformation already associated with the study of old French furniture.

As an example of this latter hazard, a commode that was sent to auction from one of the Rothschild collections was immediately accepted as the work of the famous *ébéniste* Charles Cressent (1685–1768), on the strength of a *pontil* mark in the name of that artist, the name of the family to which it had but recently belonged, and because the piece had already been published as an example of Cressent's work in a textbook on antique furniture. However, this commode was typical of many others produced during the middle of the nineteenth century, which should have been obvious, but the duplication of the Cressent mark had several times over produced the desired effect, on the susceptible purchaser, the author of the textbook, and an auction expert of many years' standing.

A more typical use of a forged *pontil* mark appeared in a collection of French furniture assembled by a well known dealer for sale at auction, following a house sale in which he as well as the auction gallery, had suffered considerable adverse criticism for loading that sale with pieces he had obtained to replace others removed by relatives of the former owner. To forestall any further repercussions, and also as it was known that my interpretations of his merchandise would be fair and equitable, I was commissioned to catalogue the collection. It included a large suite of seat furniture just brought over from France, purporting to have been made by Nogaret-à-Lyon. This suite had been formed of genuinely antique pieces, fragments of matching antique pieces, and two *banquettes* entirely of new material. These latter pieces bore exactly the same *pontil* mark as those appearing on every other piece in the set; and at my suggestion they were withdrawn from the sale. By the time of my examination, photographs for illustration in this book as representations of Nogaret's work had been ordered and received from Lyon and other museums and, along with additional examples, I was able to prove that the design of this suite did not in any way approximate any of the characteristic working styles of the *menuisier* to whom it had thus been accredited. Notwithstanding this evidence and that of the same stamp on the new *banquettes,* the gallery then dispatched one of the chairs of the set to a highly regarded specialist in French furniture, who accepted the mark as undisputably genuine, and when the sale took place bid in a part of the suite for his own clientele.

In addition to the Parisian furniture that members of the local *Communauté* did not choose to sign there was also a large unidentified output of foreigners and Protestants who were not permitted to stamp their work. Composed largely of German cabinetmakers and artists in marquetry, these craftsmen lived and worked in the suburb of Saint-Antoine, within the protection of the *Abbaye de Saint-Antoine-des-Champs* and the ancient sanctuary rights of the Catholic Church. It is apparent that many of these marquetry workers received employment in shops of recognized masters, while others maintained prosperous shops in their own section of Paris where they produced excellent furniture to sell at lower prices than those charged by accepted members of the Communauté. To counteract increasing competition between its members and unrecognized or "false" workers, in 1776 the society finally admitted Protestants to membership with the same rights as Catholics, and aliens were admitted free of naturalization fees.

The rights and privileges enjoyed by Paris masters were similarly exercised when a *menuisier* or *ébéniste* returned to his place of birth or sought to attain success in a lesser city. More often, however, these smaller furniture centres, particularly those situated in the eastern half of the country, attracted artisans from the Netherlands, the neighboring German states, Switzerland, and Italy. The talents of German marquetry workers were especially acceptable to established members of local *Communautés,* just as similar skills were appreciated in Paris.

While no other French metropolis could approach the importance of the capital city or the advances achieved there during the eighteenth century, a number of cities outranked other capitals and thriving commercial centres of Europe. It is therefore important in order to gain some idea of the amount and quality of unrecorded furniture executed in these French cities that suitable comparisons be made. Lyon was a much greater city than either the capital of Denmark or of Sweden, both of which produced furniture of outstanding merit. Marseille and Bordeaux were larger than Florence and Brussels. Lille, Nantes, and Toulouse were each more populous than Antwerp or Dresden. Both Strasbourg and Orléans overshadowed Munich; Nancy and Angers each contained a greater population than Potsdam.

Avignon, Grenoble, Aix, and Tours were larger towns than Bruges, Delft, or Stuttgart. In addition to the separate woodworking guilds established in these locals, others existed in such towns as Metz, Arles, Nîmes, Puttelange, Auxonne, Avalon, Dijon, Montbéliard, Rennes, Le Mans, Anjou, Rouen, Caen, Valenciennes, and Marly.

Ateliers of Strasbourg, Grenoble, Marseille, Bordeaux, Tours, Dijon, and Montbéliard, in particular, were responsible for the production of finely designed and executed *meubles de luxe*—often with greater structural perfection than customary in the average Parisian shop. Leading members and officials of local *Communautés* gave employment to fifteen or more shop workers, while at times additional help was necessary to meet the more urgent demands of villas owned by the nobility or wealthy citizens. Special skills in inlaid and sculptured effects were requisitioned for completing many of the more luxurious productions, for lacquer decorations carried out principally in the Chinese taste, and in the casting and finishing of gilded bronze mounts.

Internal and foreign impulses resulting in various style movements might be felt in other cities or towns at the same time or almost as soon as they were received in Paris. These forces had developed to a considerable degree during the sixteenth century, when Lyon, Dijon, Rouen, Avignon, and other cities were already famous as important furniture centres. Of the three leading designers working in France at that time, Hugues Sambin confined his skills to the vicinity of Dijon, while Jean Goujon, of Rouen, left that city to obtain greater success in Paris. There his style, both as a sculptor and designer of furniture, was recognized as possessing greater delicacy and refinement than that of the third Parisian master, Jacques Androuet du Cerceau.

The increasing movements of artists and workers to and from Paris, and general developments in all forms of communication eventually led to a wide and fairly rapid transmission of designs during the eighteenth century, particularly in the closing years of the Louis XV period. Certain forms and decorative treatments adopted or evolved by craftsmen of lesser cities were, with greater frequency than Parisian work, continued for several decades, or from one style period to another. However, many compositions may be safely dated within five or ten years of related designs executed in Paris. As few examples are actually documented in this respect especial importance is to be attached to the *boîte de maîtrise* executed by the *menuisier-ébéniste* François-Joseph Kaeshammer. A handsome sarcophagus-form *coffret* of severe architectural design, with moldings and fine relief carving in the fully developed Classic or so-called Louis XVI taste, was offered before the *Communauté des Maîtres-menuisiers français de la Ville de Strasbourg* in 1771, when the work of many Parisian masters was still motivated by Rococo designs.

In many localities and in Paris the ordinary forms of seat furniture were augmented by other forms styled to provide greater ease and luxury for writing, dressing, or other special purposes. Master joiners responsible for such work also supplied plain or richly carved bedsteads, in natural or painted finishes. The more elegant of these, surmounted by elaborate canopies, are as readily mistaken for Parisian examples as are the finer seat frames. Additionally, the *menuisier* or *menuisier-ébéniste,* sometimes in collaboration with a *sculpteur en bois,* produced centre and console tables of many forms, and also bureaus, commodes, armoires, and so on, which in general departed more noticeably from Paris examples.

Master *ébénistes* exercised their more refined talents in supplying cabinetwork that was often modeled after the latest Parisian forms of occasional tables, dressing tables, and similar types of mobile furniture. Among the heavier pieces, the *bureau plat* was furnished with a *cartonnier* soon after this convenience was adopted in Paris, though different types of *bureaux* and *secrétaires* were more universally favored, especially the *bureau à penle* and the *secrétaire à abattant.* Such pieces, as well as commodes and cabinets, of the same craftsmanship, and those mentioned above as products of the joiner, might be assembled in villas or other residences where they would be set off against handsomely molded and carved *boiseries* or room panelings. The *sculpteur en bois* was also called upon to furnish mirror framings for this woodwork, and at times mural paintings, tapestries, silk damasks, native *toiles peintes, toiles des Indes,* or other auxiliary wall treatments were introduced.

As the eighteenth century progressed marquetry techniques that were introduced or evolved in various furniture centres became increasingly cosmopolitan and in many instances approached the sophistication of Parisian accomplishments. Treatments favored by native or German-born *marqueteurs* featured landscapes, figures, birds amid foliations, urns, draperies, various attributes, clustered trophies, and groups of table utensils. A great variety of parquetry effects also came into vogue and numerous types of intricately inlaid bandings or wider borders. Performances such as these, and refinements in the work of local joiners, were made possible by a lavish repertory of native and imported timbers.

Forest and fruit trees growing in or near these localities provided abundant supplies of beech, walnut, cherry, and oak. Chestnut was found in some areas, particularly in the west of France. Elm and ash were plentiful, with burl cuttings of these timbers serving the cabinetmaker, as well as those of walnut—a timber exported from eastern provinces to England. Sycamore was frequently employed as a veneer or inlay material, while poplar, birch, locust, maple, lime, holly, and box were also accessible.

Of the numerous fruitwoods, supplies of *citronnier* were apportioned according to local requirements, those of the capital, and shipments destined for northern areas of Europe. The more strikingly marked olivewood of southern France was similarly distributed. Plumwood was frequently available for veneering or inlaid work, and also laburnum or *ébénier des Alpes,* Saint Lucie cherry, service tree, pear, apple, orange, apricot, and mulberry.

Pine was a principal medium for concealed structural work as executed in all French cities and towns. This softwood might be employed singly, or conforming with fairly common Parisian habit, in combination with oak. In rare instances oak was the sole medium of such work performed outside of the capital, a choice also eventually adopted by the finest Parisian masters of the late eighteenth century. Fir and larch were used to some extent in the east and southeast of France, and Italian poplar was occasionally used in southern localities.

To increase the effectiveness of surface panels laid upon these cores local *marqueteurs* developed secret or less carefully guarded formulas for staining or dyeing the lighter colored hardwoods. Some were given more or less brilliant red and blue tones. Others were dyed to various shades of green, especially sycamore, which thus duplicated the appearance of English "harewood." In keeping with a technique followed throughout Europe pearwood was stained to simulate ebony.

Dutch and French shipping interests in tropical America, Asia, and Africa led to the distribution of exotic timbers via Holland and the Rhine passageway, through Bordeaux where some of the largest shipments of mahogany to arrive in Europe were received during the second half of the eighteenth century, and through Lorient in the province of Bretagne, further removed from Paris than the Normandy port of Le Havre. From Bordeaux locally made furniture was dispatched to America. These arterial and sea deliveries provided *ébénistes* located in both the eastern and western portions of France with such timbers as palisander, violet wood (later to be known as kingwood or *bois du Roi*), tulipwood, amaranth, ebony, and thuja, in addition to mahogany, which at the close of the eighteenth century was first adopted by *menuisiers* specializing in seat furniture.

Through the commerce in antiques that has developed ever since the beginning of the nineteenth century, examples of furniture emanating from many other localities of France have been intermingled with those originating in the city and suburbs of Paris. Since a majority of the former pieces are unsigned, or in certain instances unrecognized marks have been removed in favor of others, and as local records have not been so carefully preserved or studied as those of Paris, there is still a very great deal to be learned about the hundreds of masters belonging to *Communautés* established throughout the country. The register attempted here is very far from a complete listing of those responsible for skills of sufficient merit to receive contemporary recognition. Further knowledge of these skills may eventually result from additional researches such as those carried out so successfully by Edmond Delaye and Jeanne Michel Giroud.

REGISTER OF MASTER *MENUISIERS* AND *ÉBÉNISTES* OF PROVINCES OTHER THAN ÎLE DE FRANCE

This is a fragmentary listing only, for instead of the ten or fifteen names here associated with each of a number of French cities, some cities contained individual quotas of well over a hundred master craftsmen located in separate establishments, quotas that were maintained throughout the greater part of the eighteenth century. In Marseille, alone, there were 151 masters working during the start of the century, and 144 were recorded there in 1782. The following abbreviations are used:

men.	*Menuisier*	gr.	Graver signature
eb.	*Ebéniste*	lab.	Printed label
marq.	*Marqueteur*	b.	Born
scu.	*Sculpteur*	r.m.	Received or recorded as master of local *Communauté*
tour.	*Tourneur*	w.	Worked as master
mach.	*Machiniste*	c.	Circa
mar'd	*Marchand*	C.	Century
pon.	*Pontil* signature	d.	Died
insc.	Inscribed signature		

NAME	LOCATION	PERIOD OR STYLE
Abraham (eb.)	Bordeaux	Louis XVI
Adam (men., pon.)	Unknown	Louis XVI b. 1720
Andriss, Sébastien (eb.)	Strasbourg	r.m. 1743
Audeville (eb.)	Nantes	Louis XVI
Bailly, Antoine (eb.)	Grenoble	Régence, Louis XV
Balthazar, François (men.)	Auxonne	Régence, Louis XV
Baron (eb.)	Nantes	Louis XV, XVI
Becquet (men.)	Rambouillet	Louis XV, XVI
Bergamin, Antoine (eb.)	Marseille	Louis XV
Bergamin, Marc-Antoine (eb.)	Marseille	Louis XVI

Name	Location	Period or Style
Bernard (eb.)	Angers	Louis XVI
Bilzig, Julien (men., insc.)	Unknown	Régence
Blanchon, P.-J. (men., pon.)	Unknown	Louis XVI
Blerouge (men., pon.)	Unknown	Louis XV
Blumer, Jean-Chrétian (men.–eb.)	Strasbourg	b.c. 1731 r.m. 1765 d. 1807
Bontan (eb.)	Lyon	Louis XVI
Boudhors, Pierre-Philippe (men.–eb.)	Strasbourg	r.m. 1780
Bourron, Pierre-Paul (eb.–tour.)	Grenoble	Louis XV, XVI
Bregueth (eb., pon.)	Unknown	Louis XVI
Bresler, Jean ("Alsace") (eb.)	Bordeaux	Louis XVI r.m. 1756
Briffault, Louis (men.–eb.)	Dijon	w. 1780
Cambon, Pierre (men.–eb.)	Avallon	Louis XV
Canot, François (men.–scu.)	Lyon	b. (Paris) c. 1721 w.c. 1748 d. 1786
Carel (eb., pon.)	Unknown	Louis XV
Carpentier, Sébastien (men., pon.)	Lyon	b. 1733 w.c. 1760 d. 1813
Casse (men.–eb.–scu.)	Bordeaux?	Louis XV
Chelant (men.)	Unknown	Louis XV
Chevallier, Michel (eb.)	Grenoble	Louis XIV, Régence
Cocke, Bernard (men.)	Strasbourg	Louis XV
Collogne (eb.)	Bordeaux	Louis XVI
Comby, Pierre (men.)	Toulouse	r.m. 1782
Cormeray, Pierre-Joachim (marc.–eb.)	Nantes	Louis XVI, Directoire
Couillaud, Jacques (eb.)	Nantes	Louis XVI
Couleru, Abraham-Nicolas (eb.–marq.)	Montbéliard	b. 1716 r.m. 1750 d. 1812
Couleru, Georges-David (eb.)	Montbéliard	b. 1761 d. 1845
Couleru, Marc-David (eb.)	Montbéliard	b. 1731 d. 1804
Couleru, Pierre-Nicolas (eb.)	Montbéliard	b. 1755 d. 1824
Courtoy, J.-M. (men., pon.)	Unknown	Louis XV
Cruchet, Gabriel (men.)	Tours	r.m. 1748 w. 1787+

Name	Location	Period or Style
Debergue, François (men.)	Valenciennes	Louis XV
Delaurier (eb.)	Strasbourg	Louis XV, XVI
Demoulin, Jean (eb., pon.)	Dijon	b. 1715 r.m. 1780 d. 1798
Demoulin, Les Frères (eb's., pon.)	Dijon	Louis XVI w. to 19th C.
Denotte, Jean (men.)	Tours	r.m. 1753 w. to 1775+
Dicop, Nicolas (eb.)	Metz	Louis XVI
Dimanche, Henry (eb.)	Metz	Louis XVI, Directoire
Dubois (eb.)	Bordeaux	Louis XVI
Dubois, J. (men.–eb.)	Le Mans	Louis XV, XVI
Du Breuilhy (marq., gr.)	Orléans	Louis XVI
Dugardin, L. (eb., pon.)	Unknown	Louis XV
Durand, Hugues (eb.)	Grenoble	Louis XV
Érard, Antoine (men.)	Strasbourg	Louis XV, XVI
Érard, Louis-Antoine (men.)	Strasbourg	Louis XV
Escoffier, Étienne (eb.)	Grenoble	Régence
Fontaine (eb.)	Rouen	19th c.–Louis XVI
Fontaine, F. C. (eb.)	Unknown	Louis XVI
Fougère (eb.)	Metz	Louis XVI
Fournier, N. C. (men., pon.)	Unknown	Louis XV
Froy de Veau, René (eb., insc.)	Strasbourg	b. 1727 r.m. 1758 d. 1802
Fustig, R.-M. (marq., gr.)	Unknown	Louis XVI
Gailliard (eb., insc.)	Orléans	Louis XVI
Gardin, Jean (mar'd–eb.)	Marseille	Louis XVI
Garrée, J.-F. (eb., pon.)	Unknown	Louis XVI
Gautier, Jean (eb.)	Strasbourg	Louis XV
Geny, François (men., pon.)	Lyon	b. (Paris) 1731 w. (Lyon) c. 1752 d. 1804
George (mar'd–eb.)	Toulouse	Louis XVI
Gerboud, Claude (eb.)	Lyon	b. 1736 d. 1800
Gouiran, Louis (eb.)	Marseille	Louis XV
Gruyer, J. (eb., pon.)	Unknown	Louis XVI
Guénerie (men.)	Nantes	Louis XVI
Guérard, Joseph (eb.)	Bordeaux	Louis XVI
Guérin (men.–mach., pon.)	Montpellier	Louis XV
Guillat, Claude-Alexis (eb.)	Grenoble	Louis XV, XVI
Guillaume (men.)	Metz	Louis XVI

Name	Location	Period or Style
Hache, Christophe-André (men.–eb., lab.)	Grenoble	b. 1748 d. 1831
Hache, Jean-François (men.–eb., pon., lab.)	Grenoble	b. 1730 d. 1800
Hache, Pierre (men.–eb., pon.)	Grenoble	b. 1703 d. 1776
Hache, Thomas (men.–eb.)	Grenoble	b. 1664 d. 1747
Hay, Jacques (eb.)	Avignon	Louis XIV
Hilaire, Georges (eb.)	Tours	Louis XVI
Hubert, Jean (eb.)	Grenoble	Louis XIV
Hue, Philippe (men.)	Caen	Louis XVI
Irmann, Jean-Daniel (men.)	Strasbourg	Louis XV, XVI
Javoy, Claude (men.–eb.)	Nantes	r.m. (Paris) 1779 w. (Nantes) c. 1783+
Joly, Jean-Alexandre (eb.)	Nancy	r.m. 1786
Kaeshammer, François de Paule-Joseph (men.–eb.–scu.)	Strasbourg	b. 1747 r.m. 1771 w. to 19th C.
Keres (eb.)	Marseille	Louis XVI
Klein, R. C. (eb.–marq.)	Unknown	Louis XV
Kocke, Bernard (men.–eb.)	Strasbourg	r.m. 1741
Krieg, Michel (men.)	Orléans	r.m. 1769 w. to Revolution
Krier, Jean (men.)	Puttelange	Louis XV
Labourier (eb.)	Bordeaux	Louis XVI
Lamy, René (men.)	Tours	Louis XV, XVI
Lapierre, François (men., pon.)	Lyon	b. 1753 w.c. 1780 d. 1813
Laroze (eb.)	Bordeaux	Louis XVI
Lavocat (men.–mach.)	Champigneulles	Louis XVI
Lebattu, Jean (men.)	Nantes	Louis XVI
Lebrund (Jean-Baptiste Topino) (mar'd–eb., pon.)	Marseille	Louis XVI
Lemasle (eb.)	Nantes	Louis XVI
Lemasle, Les Frères (eb's.)	Nantes	Directoire
Lemée, Jean (men.)	Unknown	Louis XVI
Levet, Claude (men.–scu.)	Lyon	b. 1729 w.c. 1753 d. 1774
Lhumot, Barthélemy (eb.)	Nancy	r.m. 1786
Loison (men., insc.)	Unknown	Louis XVI
Longbois (men.)	Lyon	18th C.

Name	Location	Period or Style
Lutel (men.–eb., pon.)	Unknown	Louis XV
Mahé, V.-B.-E. (men., pon.)	Unknown	Louis XVI
Mathalm ("Lefranc") (eb.)	Bordeaux	Louis XVI
Maubossin (men.)	La Suze (Maine)	Louis XVI
Maurice, L. (men., pon.)	Unknown	Louis XV
Mayran, Guillaume (eb.)	Grenoble	Régence
Meyerdietrich, Jean (men.–scu.)	Strasbourg	r.m. 1767 w. to Revolution
Miller, Nicolas (eb.)	Nancy	r.m. 1788
Mirland, R. (eb., pon.)	Unknown	Louis XVI
Moulinet, Pierre (men.)	Tours	r.m. 1751 d. 1784
Muller (eb.)	Nancy	Louis XVI
Nicolas, Michel (men.–eb.)	Tours	r.m. 1764 w. to Revolution
Nogaret, Pierre (men., pon.)	Lyon	B. (Paris) c. 1720 r.m. (Lyon) 1745 d. 1771
Oeben, Joseph ("Open") (eb., pon.)	Tours	r.m. 1781 w. to Revolution
Open, J., *see* Oeben, Joseph		
Parmentier, Sebastien (men.)	Meurthe	Louis XV
Parmentiers, Les (pon.):		
Parmentier À Lyon		
Parmentier, Antoine (men.)	Lyon	b. 1772 w.c. 1799-1815
Parmentier, Claude (men.)	Lyon	b.c. 1754 w. 1775+
Parmentier, Nicolas (men.)	Lyon	b.c. 1736 m. 1768 d. 1801
Peff (eb.)	Nancy	Louis XVI
Peifer (eb.–marq.)	Metz	Louis XVI
Picot, Grégoire (eb.)	Nancy	Louis XVI
Pill, Pierre (eb.–marq.)	Tours	Louis XV, XVI
Pillot (men.–eb., pon.)	Nîmes	Louis XVI
Piqueret, Isaac (eb.–marq.)	Avignon	Louis XIV
Pollet, M. (men., pon.)	Unknown	Louis XV
Provot (men.–eb.)	Nancy	Louis XVI
Renault, René (men.)	Tours	r.m. 1747 w. 1775+
Reni (eb.)	Nîmes	w. 1755+
Reuse (eb., pon.)	Unknown	Louis XV
Rochon (mar'd–eb.)	Bordeaux	Louis XVI

Name	Location	Period or Style
Roetters, Gaspard (eb.–marq.)	Tours	Louis XV, XVI
Roetters, Bertrand (eb.–marq.)	Tours	Louis XV, XVI
Rommécourt (men., pon.)	Unknown	Directoire
Roussens, J.-I. (men., pon.)	Unknown	Louis XVI
Saddon, J. (eb., pon.)	Unknown	Louis XV
Saverau, Aimé (eb.)	Nantes	Louis XV
Sengens, J. (eb., pon.)	Unknown	Louis XV
Tanner, T. A. (men., pon.)	Unknown	Louis XVI
Thomas, Joseph (eb.)	Dijon	Louis XVI
Thullier, Charles (eb.)	Nancy	r.m. 1787
Tillot, Jean-Baptiste (eb.)	Grenoble	Régence Louis XV
Tissier (eb.)	Unknown	Louis XV
Topino, Jean-Baptiste, *see* Lebrund		
Tournai (eb.)	Bordeaux	Louis XV
Trille (men.)	Toulouse	Louis XV, XVI
Vaugry, Jean (men.–scu.)	Unknown	Louis XV
Vesco, Martin-Joseph (eb.)	Metz	b. 1763 r.m. 1787 d. 1814
Wime, H. (eb., pon.)	Unknown	Régence
Zettler, Georges (eb., insc.)	Marseille	Late 18th C.

During the eighteenth century many ateliers or warerooms were operated by *marchands* who may or may not have been qualified as *menuisiers* or *ébénistes*. Around the close of the century establishments of this description appear to have been especially popular in Marseille, where among many other proprietors the more carefully transcribed listings include the names of Jean Beauquety, Jean Bogmas, Jean Bourcard, Henry Casemer, Marcel Ducret, Guillaume Elbert, Charles Frédéric, Joseph Graf, Gaspard Houpp, Étienne Reynard, François Reynard, Frédéric Roudard, and Bernard Sarri.

VOCABULARY OF FRENCH TERMS
APPLIED TO EIGHTEENTH-CENTURY FURNITURE

abattant. Hinged leaf or panel of a writing cabinet or table, dropping forward in opening; a *tablette* (Lucotte). Sometimes used in reference to a leaf of a drop-leaf table.

accotoir. Arm rest. See *accoudoir.*

accoudoir. Arm or elbow of a chair, generally with an armpad or *manchette;* also the crest rail of a *voyeuse,* when padded *accoudoir* or *accotoir à manchette.* See *bras.*

ambulante. Portable stand or table, generally for serving purposes.

ameublement. Furniture, *meubles.*

anneau. Ring handle.

applique. Bracket, wall sconce.

archelle. Hanging shelf for vases, utensils, and so forth, as used in northern France.

armoire. Cupboard or press with one or two full-length doors, or in two sections as an *armoire à deux corps.*

armoire à bijoux. Jewel cabinet.

armoire à deux corps. See *armoire.*

armoire à glace. Cabinet with glazed door or doors.

armoire basse. Low case with one or more doors; *bas d'armoire.*

armoire d'encoignure. Corner *armoire.* See *cantonnière.*

armoire de lin. Linen cupboard or press.

armoire en corbeille. *Armoire* with corbeled shaping in the lower body.

armoire galbée. *Armoire* with swept or serpentine front shaping.

assemblage. Joining methods.

astragale. Astragal or mullion.

atelier. Workshop or factory. *L'atelier d'un menuisier:* joiner's workshop.

athénienne. Usually a tetrapod to hold a *jardinière.*

baguette. Quarter- or half-round molding. Glass prism or luster.

baguette de lauriers. Convex molding of imbricated laurel leaves.

bahut. Chest or trunk, often with a barrel lid. A low cupboard (of northern France) with one or two drawers above double doors.

bahutier. Maker of *bahuts* or *coffres,* trunk-maker.

baignoire. Stool, chair, or long seat fitted with a basin or tub (Delafosse) (Roubo). Bathtub.

balancier. Pendulum of a clock.

baldaquin. Canopy over a bed or chair, generally semicircular in plan.

balustre. Baluster or upright support.

banc. Bench, with or without a back.

bandeau. Band or fillet.

bandelette. Narrow band or fillet.

banquette. Long stool or bench, with or without end *dossiers.*

banquette de croisée. Window seat of usual size or longer (Delafosse).

barbière. Shaving stand or table.

baromètre à cadran. Barometer with dial plate, generally set off against an upright ornamental panel.

baromètre à cuvette. Cistern barometer.

baromètre à siphon. Siphon barometer.

Baroque Style. Baroque Style The Baroque, in its final stage as a movement leading up to the refinements of the Rococo period, was a style characterized by "dynamic opposition, and energy, and by the use of curved and contorted forms"—frequently combined with plainer lines or structural elements.

barrière. Footboard or low barrier of a bed, as in many rural examples.

bas d'armoire. Low *meuble* of commode size or larger but with one or more doors; generally used in reference to metropolitan pieces.

bas de buffet. Low cupboard, similar in form to the lower section of a *buffet à deux corps;* applied to pieces of either rustic or finished craftsmanship.

berceau. Cradle.

berceuse. Anchor-form rocking chair (Delafosse).

bergère. Upholstered or caned easy chair with low closed sides.

bergère à joues. Easy chair with upholstered or caned back and wings, or cheeks.

bergère à oreilles. Easy chair with upholstered or caned back and wings, or ears.

bergère en confessional. *Bergère* with winged sides.

bergère en gondole. *Bergère* with round-arched horseshoe back.

bibliothèque. Bookcase, bookshelves, library; *armoire* or cabinet with doors generally containing *grillage*—or latticework in metal or wood; in either one or two stages (Lucotte). *Petit bibliothèque:* open-shelf cabinet with cupboard below (Lucotte).

bidet. A night stool: with narrow back (*siège d'aisances*) (Roubo), with *dossier* containing a screen or mriror, or supporting a shelf for toilet articles (Delafosse).

Bois. Wood, timber. *Bois d'acacia, bois de rose, bois des Indes,* and so on, as listed below:

acacia. Acacia.

acajou. Mahogany; *acajou moucheté:* plum-pudding mahogany.

alisier. Whitebeam.

amarante. Amaranth.

amboine. Amboina wood.

aubour. Laburnum.

aune. Alder.

boissant. Lignum vitae.

bouleau. Birch.

buis. Boxwood.

cèdre. Cedar.

cerisier. Cultivated cherry.

charme. Hornbeam, yoke elm.
châtaignier. Chestnut.
chêne. Oak.
citronnier. Citron or lemon wood.
clairembourg. Fustic.
corail. Red sandalwood.
cormier. Service tree.
coudrier. Hazel.
courbaril. Tropical American locust.
ébène de Portugal. Mauritius ebony.
ébène vert. Green ebony.
érable. Maple; *érable moucheté:* bird's-eye maple; *broussin d'érable:* burl maple.
faux acacia. Locust.
faux ébénier. Laburnum.
frêne. Ash; *loupe de frêne:* burl ash; *frêne vert:* green ash.
fusain. Spindle tree.
fustet. Venetian sumac.
fustoc. Fustic.
genévrier. Juniper.
hêtre. Beech.
houx. Holly.
if. Yew; *racine d'if:* yew burl.
Indes. Any wood imported from the West or East Indies.
jaune. *Satiné jaune,* see *satiné.*
marronnier de l'Inde. Horse chestnut.
mélèze. Larch.
merisier. Wild cherry.
mûrier. Mulberry.
noisetier. Hazel.
nord. Fir, spruce.
noyer. Walnut: *loupe de noyer:* burl walnut.
olivier. Olivewood.
orange. Fustic.
oranger. Bitter orange.
orme. Elm; *loupe d'orme:* burl elm.
ozier. Willow.
palissandre. Palisander.
peuplier. Poplar.
pir. Pine.
pitch-pin. Pitch pine.
platane. Plane tree.
poirier. Pearwood.
pommier. Applewood.
prunier. Plumwood.
Rhodes. Rhodeswood, or amyris.

roi. Violet wood, or (19th-20th century) kingwood.

rose. Tulipwood.

santal citrin. Sandalwood.

santal rouge. Red sandalwood, or ruby wood.

sapin. Fir, spruce.

satine. Satinwood; *bois satiné* is also used in reference to various woods or veneeers with satin finishes, including *satiné jaune:* fustic (*Chlorophora tinctoria*), and *satiné rouge* (*Brosimum paraense*).

sorbier. Service tree.

sureau. Elder.

sycomore. Sycamore.

thuya. Thuja.

tilleul. Limewood.

violet. Violet wood, or (19th-20th century) *bois du roi.*

bois clair. Wood of a natural light tone.

bois de bout. Transversely-cut veneers or "oystering," usually of violet wood, used in marquetry work.

bois de couleurs. Naturally colored or artificially tinted wood veneers; *marqueterie de b. de c.*

bois naturel. Wood with the natural color showing beneath a clear finish, as often found in joiners' pieces made of local timbers.

boisage. Woodwork.

boiserie. Wainscot, wainscoting, wood paneling.

boîte. Box, *coffret,* case.

boîte à chandelles. Candlebox.

boite à farine. An open hanging box, apparently to contain flour or meal without protection from dust—or candles.

boîte à musique. Music box.

boîte à ouvrage. Workbox.

boîte de maîtrise. A box or *coffret* at times made for the acceptance piece of an apprentice craftsman.

boîte d'horloge. Case in the form of a pedestal or *gaine,* containing a clock (Delafosse).

boîte de pendule. Clock in pedestal-form case, or bracket clock with bracket (Lucotte) (Roubo); tall-case clock (Roubo).

bonheur du jour. Lady's writing table with recessed superstructure, a *table à gradin;* also, when the cabinet section is meant for display purposes, a *table à vitrine.*

bonnetière. Narrow *armoire* or cupboard with single door, generally of solid construction, the width commensurate with a very wide bonnet.

bout de pied. End or foot section of a *chaise longue* or *duchesse brisée.*

bouton. Stud or button, as in various decorative uses.

bras. Arm, as of a chair or *canapé.* An early form of armchair may be referred to as a *chaise à bras,* or *chaise à bras sans manchettes* when the arms are not fitted with armpads.

buffet. Cupboard or sideboard with a door or doors, and often with one or more drawers; generally used in reference to a piece taller than the *buffet bas.* A regular cupboard in either one or two sections (Roubo) (Lucotte) (Delafosse).

buffet à deux corps. Cupboard in two stages.

buffet à glissants. As popularly made in Provence, a low cupboard or *credence* in the form of a *buffet bas* but with low recessed plateau enclosed by sliding front panels. See *tirette.*

buffet-bahut. As made in Auvergne, a cupboard in two stages, each enclosed by a pair of doors separated by a central stile.

buffet bas. Low cupboard of approximately the form given to the lower section of a *buffet à deux corps.*

buffet-crédence. Low buffet, *buffet bas,* or *buffet à glissants.*

buffet de salle à manger. Dresser, of suburban or rural type.

buffet-scriban. Secretary cabinet with slant-front writing section.

buffet-servante. *Meuble* of commode height and plan, but with open shelves at either end; generally of metropolitan work influenced by English designs.

buffet-vaisselier. Open dresser for dishes, with lower enclosed cupboard section; widely popular in suburban and rural areas. A *vaisselier.*

bureau. Writing table, desk. Pedestal desk with recessed kneehole portion—somewhat similar to English forms (Lucotte).

bureau à caissona. Kneehole writing table, with shallow central, and deeper end sections; *b. à c. lateraux.*

bureau à cylindre. Cylinder-front writing table with solid or tambour cylinder; *secrétaire à panse.*

bureau à dos d'âne. Slant-front writing table, the sides of vertical serpentine contours and rounded at the top; *secrétaire en tombeau.* For varying designs with straight sides see *bureau à pente.*

bureau à pente. Slant-front writing table of average form, the sides generally accepted as being flat. A *secrétaire* (Lucotte) (Roubo).

bureau à pupitre. Table with central writing easel.

bureau-bibliothèque. Desk surmounted by a cabinet section for books.

bureau de dame. Lady's writing table or desk.

bureau de milieu. Writing table or heavier desk finished on all four sides.

bureau galbé. See *galbe.*

bureau plat. Writing table with flat top.

bureau-scriban. Slant-front bureau, a form developed to some extent in provinces adjacent to the Netherlands and the English Channel.

cabaret. Liquor case.

cabinet. Cabinet; closet, study, cabinet, office.

cabriolet. See *chaise en cabriolet.*

cadre. Frame, for a mirror or picture.

canapé. Settee, caned or upholstered; with open arms (Delafosse) (Lucotte). *Demi-canapé:* small settee. See *sofa.*

canapé à console. Settee with projecting seat front supported by a central leg of console form (Delafosse) (Lucotte).

canapé à corbeille. Settee or *sofa* with arched horseshoe frame, the sides curving in at the seat front.

canapé à joues. Settee with lateral wings or cheeks.

canne. Cane or caning, as used for a *siège de canne* or *chaise cannée.*

cannelures. Flutes, grooves, fluting.

cannelures avec rudentures. Flutings with cable fillets: *cannelures rudentèes.*

cantonnière. Bed or window valance.

cantonnière. Corner *armoire* of Provence, also known as a *cantouniero.*

carreaux. Movable pads for the backs and seats of rushed or caned chairs.

cartel. Wall clock.

cartonnier. Nest of cardboard boxes or cartons (*cartonniers*), serving as drawers and generally faced with tooled leather. Often in an open case incorporating or supporting a clock (*pendule à cartonnier*). Used on one end of a writing table, or beside the table on a separate stand (*meuble avec cartonnier*) or on a low cupboard (*armoire de bout de bureau et cartonnier*). *Meuble-cartonnier:* a case fitted with cartons and a cupboard section of regular drawers. See *secrétaire à archives* (Lalonde).

casier. Set of pigeonholes; cupboard.

casier à musique. Open shelves to contain sheets of music.

cassette. Casket, *coffret,* small box, cash box.

causeuse. Wide upholstered chair; love seat or small sofa.

caverne. Normandy bed (*lit-clos*) of solid and partially open wood panels, one in front fitted so as to slide open and shut.

chaffeuse. Chair with low seat, as used by a fireplace.

chaise à dossier crossé. Chair with crosiered back.

chaise à dossier en balustre. Chair with back containing turned balusters or spindles.

chaise à dossier en éventail. Chair with back centering a fan splat.

chaise à dossier en médaillon. Chair with oval back. See other forms under *dossier.*

chaise à dossier enroule. Chair with out-curved or out-scrolled back.

chaise à jeu. Chair for use at a gaming table; *siège à jeu.*

chaise à la capucine. See *siège à la capucine.*

chaise à la reine. Chair with flat oval or shield-shaped back, varying from the concave form of the *chaise en cabriolet.*

chaise à oreilles. Chair with ears or wings; *confessionnal.*

chaise à porteur. Porter's hall chair.

chaise à porteurs. Sedan chair.

chaise "bonne femme." Rural type of lady's chair, generally with partially turned frame and rush seat; often fitted with *carreaux. Fauteuil "bonne femme."*

chaise de paille. Chair with rush or straw seat.

chaise de salle à manger. Dining-room chair.

chaise en cabriolet. Chair with back of concave form, in cartouche-shaped, shield, or oval vertical shapings.

chaise en gondole. Side chair or armchair with deeply concave back. See *bergère en gondole.*

chaise en vis-à-vis. Conversation or straddle chair; *chaise en contrepartie.*

chaise longue. Long chair-form seat or daybed.

chaise montgolfière. Chair with balloon back and conforming radial splat —named after the two brothers who invented the first air-balloon let off in Paris, August 27, 1783.

chaise paysanne. Peasant chair; tavern-type side chair of Alsace.

chaise percée. Chair with hinged seat above an aperture for a basin, close stool, *chaise* or *siège d'affaires.*

chaise-voyeuse. See *voyeuse.*

chambranle. Mantel; *chambranle de cheminée* (Delafosse).

chandelle à cannelures. Ornamental fillet or cable fluting.

chapelet. Pearl molding.

chapiteau. Heading, dome, crest, capital.

charpentier. Carpenter.

chauffe-assiette. Plate warmer.

chauffe-linge. Linen warmer.

chauffe-lit. Bed warmer.

chauffe-pieds. Foot warmer.

chausson. Shoe; *bronze doré* toe mount or toe cap, as fitted on cabriole legs. See *sabot*—a term preferred by some authorities in connection with the toe sockets fitted on straight legs.

chef-d'œuvre. Trial piece or masterpiece. See *pièce de maîtrise.*

cheminée. Mantelpiece, including the mantel or *chambranle,* and the *trumeau* section (Delafosse).

chenet. Firedog, andiron; by extension *not* a device for holding wood but a metal fixture or separate ornament used in front of a firedog.

cheval. A horse; hence, a support or frame.

chiffonnière. *Chiffonnier,* tall chest of drawers; small oblong table with bank of two or three drawers (Lucottte).

chinoiserie. Chinese articles on furniture, dress, porcelain, and so on, in an ornamental use; decorative composition in the Chinese taste.

chute. Pendant in the form of leafage, and so on, employed as a stile capital, and generally of gilded bronze.

ciel. Bed tester or canopy. See *plafond.*

coffre. Chest, coffer.

coffret. Small check-type box.

coffretier. Trunk-maker.

coiffeuse. Dressing table. See *poudreuse.*

coin. Corner, angle; hanging corner shelves with lower cupboard section (Lucotte).

coin du feu. Fireside sofa with angular or rounded back, the size of a *demi-canapé* or larger.

colonne. Column, pillar; bedpost, *quenouille, pilier.*

colonnette. Small column.

commode. Chest of drawers. Sometimes used in reference to a piece of commode size and shape but with cupboard space enclosed by a door or doors—preferably designated as a *meuble d'entredeux.*

commode à la Régence. Commode of serpentine or corbeled form in the spirit of the Régence period, made at least until the middle of the eighteenth century.

commode à pieds. Chest of drawers with legs of greater than average height, usually containing only two long drawers—a *petit commode* (Roubo).

commode à plan trapézoïdal. Commode with incurvate ends, usually reflecting English influence in the overall design.

commode en console. Commode of corbeled form, as a *commode à la Régence.*

commode en demi-lune. Commode of semi-elliptical plan.

commode en tombeau. Commode with protuberant side and front shapings, as a *commode à la Régence* and *c. en console.*

commode ouverte à l'anglaise. Open-shelf case (or *desserte*), in the English manner.

Communauté. Community, society, guild.

confessionnal. Wing chair; *chaise à oreilles.*

confident. Small *canapé* for two persons, partially facing in conversation. Long *canapé* with chair-form compartments at either end (Lalonde); an earlier design (Louis XV) of the same form: *canapé à joue* (Delafosse).

console. Wall bracket, corbel; solid, half-round bracket of architectural design (Lucotte).

console. Pier table, bracket-form side table with one or more legs. Various authorities prefer *table-console, table de trumeau, meuble de salon,* and so on, for oblong side tables.

console d'accoudoir. Scrolled arm support.

console en cul-de-lampe. Side table with single support, or with two or more supports joining below to produce a bracket-like effect.

coquillage. Shell work, shell-like ornament.

coquillier. Cabinet of shells.

couche. Couch, bed, bedstead.

couche à l'antique. Daybed or bedstead of Greek or Roman form.

couronne de lit. Crown of a bed canopy.

crédence. Early sideboard containing small cupboards, raised on supports joined by a platform or "pot shelf." A credence table. Low buffet with one or two doors. See *buffet bas, buffet à glissants.*

crémaillère. Trammel, adjustable pothook for a fireplace crane.

croisettes. *Ressauts,* projecting corners of frames or panel moldings, keyed corners.

cul-de-lampe. Wall sconce with console-form light arm. Architectural wall bracket (Delafosse).

demi-canapé. Small *canapé* for two persons; various forms shown by Delafosse and Lucotte. See *marquise.*

demi-cannelures alternées de feuillage. An ornamental treatment favored during the Louis XVI period, especially in gilded bronze frieze work fashioned as open flutes alternating with vertical leaf stems.

denticules. Dentils.

desserte. Serving table, or low open-face cabinet with undershelf or shelves

—often showing English influence; *servante.* The term sometimes applies to a *meuble* or *buffet de salle à manger.*

dessus de porte. Overdoor.

dossier. Chair back; headboard of a bed.

dossier en violon. Violin-shaped or panduriform back. For other descriptions of shaped *dossiers* see under *chaise.*

dressoir. Dresser, sideboard.

duchesse. Daybed or *chaise longue* with chair-form ends.

duchesse à bateau. Boat- or gondola-shaped *chaise longue.*

duchesse brisée. *Chaise longue* in two or three parts.

duchesse brisée en deux. *Chaise longue* in two parts (Delafosse).

duchesse brisée en trois. *Chaise longue* in three parts (Delafosse).

ébéniste. Cabinetmaker.

ébéniste-marchand. Cabinetmaker also acting as a merchant dealing in his own and/or other furniture.

ébéniste-marqueteur. Cabinetmaker qualified as a marquetry worker.

ébénisterie. Cabinetwork, cabinetmaking, beautifully finished woodwork, work displaying the art of the cabinetmaker rather than that of the joiner. See *menuiserie.*

écran. Screen; fire screen: *écran à feu;* screen with step or kneeling platform: *écran à marchepied.* See *paravent.*

écran-sécretaire. Cheval screen supporting a desk section.

écrin. Jewel case or casket.

écritoire. Inkstand; small drawer or compartment fitted for pen and ink.

églomisé. Reverse printing on the undersurface of a glass panel.

égouttoir. Plate rack with spindle or fret galleries, popular in Bretagne.

encadrement. Frame, cadre, framing.

en-cas. Small table with drawers or cupboard, easily portable for convenient use.

encoignure. Corner-cabinet, -cupboard, or -buffet; frequently used in reference to a low case piece other than *meuble d'encoignure* for a tall piece. A corner piece such as a table or hanging shelves. An article of seat furniture designed for a corner (Delafosse).

enroulement de rubans. Spiraled ribbon molding.

entrée de surrure. Keyhole escutcheon.

entrelacs. Interlacing ornament, as *entrelacs de rubans.*

escabeau. Early joined stool, or one of simple or early design made during the eighteenth century.

espagnolette. Capital ornament modeled as a female head and bust, popular during the Régence and early Louis XV periods, and frequently employed in *bronze doré* stile mounts of commodes or other case pieces.

espagnolette. Metal bar door fastening, or *crémone,* used as a center stay of double-doored cabinets.

estagné or *estagnie.* A set of open shelves for displaying pewter, either of standing or hanging form; especially popular in Provence.

étagère. Open shelves, either standing or hanging; dresser; whatnot.

étiquette. Label.

facette. Small panel, plane or surface.

fauteuil. Armchair, elbow chair; sometimes used interchangeably with *bergère.* See also *chaise* and *siège.*

fauteuil à coiffeuse. Dressing chair with arms.

fauteuil canné. Caned armchair.

fauteuil d'enfant. Child's chair.

fauteuil de bureau. Writing or desk chair; *fauteuil de cabinet.*

fauteuil de bureau à tournant. Writing chair, with swivel seat, *fauteuil de bureau à siège tournant, fauteuil de bureau à pivot.*

fauteuil de cabinet. Louis XV style *bergère* with arched horseshoe frame, two cabriole legs at either side, one at the rear, and one in front (Roubo). Louis XVI style *bergère* (Lalond); *chaise de cabinet* (Delafosse).

fauteuil de toilette. Dressing armchair or easy chair.

fauteuil en cabriolet. Armchair with concave back; see *chaise en cabriolet. Bergère* with concave oval back (Delafosse).

fauteuil mécanique à roulettes. Mechanically propelled invalid's chair, as made by the *menuisier-machiniste.*

feuille de placage. Veneer; *feuille pour l'ébénisterie.*

feuilles. Leaves, *feuillage:* leafage. *Feuilles d'acanthe:* acanthus leaves. *Feuilles d'eau:* water leaves. *Feuillage et perles:* foliage or bellflower motifs alternating with pearls (a favorite Classic treatment).

filets verts. Banding fillets in green or green-tinted veneers.

flambeau. Candlestick, torch, luminary.

fontaine. Fountain, cistern; urn for water, tea, and so on.

fontaine-lavabo. Wood *tablette* or bracket supporting a fountain and stand for washbasin.

gaine. Pedestal.

galbe. Entasis, sweep, swept contour; applied to bold serpentine shapings.

galerie. Gallery, as a three-quarter surround of *bronze doré* enclosing the top surface of a table or commode.

garde-manger. Livery cupboard, larder, or *armoire.*

garde-robe. Armoire or cupboard for clothes, wardrobe.

girandole. Branched candleholder, wall bracket with candle arms.

glace. Plate glass, mirror (*miroir*).

grand. Large, grand, tall, broad; as *grand lit de repos, grande armoire.*

grillage. Latticework.

guéridon. Circular or oval table or stand of medium or small size, sometimes with a shelf; a term applied to numerous forms of the Louis XVI and later style periods; also *grand guéridon,* when the diameter is greater than that of an average *table-bouillottte.* See *table à l'antique, table à déjeuner, table-guéridon.* Tripod stand of pedestal form, or a pedestal (Delafosse).

guéridon porte-lumière. Stand with candle arm or arms.

guirlande. Garland, wreath.

horloge. Clock. Sometimes preferred in reference to early clocks of small size, and tall-case clocks of suburban or rural provenance. Applicable to any clock made by the *horloger* or clockmaker. See *pendule,* and *régulateur.*

horloge rustique. Rural bracket- or tall-case clock.

huche. Kneading trough, corn bin, hutch, bin, chest. See *pétrin.*

huche à pain. Bread chest.

huchier. Early carpenter (*charpentier*) or joiner.

huchier-menuisier. Early maker of chests, stools, and other joined work; carpenter-joiner.

JME. Abbreviation for *Jurande-* or *Jures-Menuisiers-Ébénistes*—Jury or Jurors of Joiners and Cabinetmakers belonging to a *Communauté* of woodworkers.

jardinière. Flower-stand or -table.

joncs. Reeds, rushes; *joncs enrubannés:* fasciate or entwined reedings, as used in classic moldings.

laque. Lacquer, lacquered work.

lavabo. Washstand.

lectrin. See *lutrin.*

liseuse. Reading table.

lit. Bedstead, bed.

lit à colonnes. Tall-post bedstead; *lit à haut piliers; lit à quenouilles.*

lit à deux chevets. Bedstead with two headings or *dossiers.*

lit à dossiers droits. As above; also, a *lit-divan.*

lit à haut piliers. See *lit à colonnes.*

lit à parade. Bedstead for receiving callers, state bed.

lit à pavillon. Bedstead with pavilion-like or tentlike canopy.

lit à quenouilles. See *lit à colonnes.*

lit à trois dossiers. Bedstead with back and two end *dossiers;* sometimes supplied with a canopy, see below.

lit à la chinoise. Any bedstead in the Chinese taste. Open bedstead, or with two *dossiers,* a canopy at the head or centered above, with ornamentation in the Chinese taste (Delafosse).

lit à la duchesse. State bedstead with heading draped and surmounted by a projecting curtained canopy.

lit à la français. Bedstead with low heading (or paneled above this single *dossier*) to be placed against a wall, the canopy projecting to the open front and hung with a valance, side and rear curtains (Delafosse) (Roubo); similar, but with two *dossiers* (Lucotte); with single *dossier* and four columns supporting a serpentine-arched canopy (Roubo).

lit à l'italienne. A *lit à trois dossiers,* surmounted by a canopy with curtains gathered at the wall side or at the centers of the end *dossiers* (Delafosse). Open bedstead with single *dossier,* and canopy above projecting forward to the foot, supported by two pendant brackets (Lucotte; repeated by Roubo as a *lit de repos*).

lit à la polonaise. A *lit à trois dossiers* with canopy supported by slanting, covered iron rods (Delafosse) (Lucotte); with corner uprights of the end *dossiers* continuing to slender tall posts supporting an oblong tester with central dome (Lalonde).

lit à la turque. Bedstead with two serpentine out-scrolled *dossiers* (Roubo); or with two shaped but not out-scrolled *dossiers* and a crown-shaped canopy centered above with curtains gathered on the wall side (Delafosse).

lit-clos. Paneled wood bedstead, the outer side constructed to open and close, with air admitted through decorative apertures or rows of spindle turnings. *Lit demi-clos:* a similar form but with the outer face partially open, and sometimes with a curtain replacing the sliding or removable panels of the *lit-clos.* Both forms popular in Bretagne, as in other cold and damp areas of Europe.

lit d'alcôve. In the more sophisticated designs generally a *lit à dossiers droits* or *lit de travers,* although some eighteenth-century drawings show alcoves with bedsteads projecting forward rather than placed in the usual lateral position, at times with single, elaborated headings.

lit d'ange. *Lit à dossiers droits,* the one heading surmounted by a projecting valanced tester with curtains gathered at either side of a hanging drapery panel.

lit de bout. Bedstead with single *dossier,* the foot open between two short posts or curved uprights; also shown with a heading of usual height, and a lower *dossier* at the foot.

lit de jour. Daybed, either upholstered or caned.

lit de parade. See *lit à parade.*

lit de repos. Daybed, couch, a full-size single bedstead with two *dossiers:* with three *dossiers,* as a *lit en canapé* (Delafosse). A single bed with one *dossier* (Lucotte) (Roubo).

lit de repos à la romaine. Récamier-type sofa.

lit de repos à la turque. Bedstead with single *dossier,* the *montants* voluted (Lalonde).

lit de travers. Similar to the *lit à dossiers droits* and the usual form of the *lit d'alcôve,* generally with one or both side rails enriched. *Lit de travers à chevets droits.*

lit en bateau. Boat- or gondola-shaped bedstead.

lit en canapé. *Lit à trois dossiers,* following the lines of a *canapé; lit-canapé.*

lit en tombeau. *Lit à trois dossiers,* with slanting tester.

lutrin. Lectern; music, reading, or writing desk with pillar support.

machiniste. Machinist, mechanic, one skilled in the use of machine tools.

maie. Kneading trough, flour bin; *pétrin*—also known in Provence as a *mastro.*

main de tirage. Drawer pull or handle.

maître ébéniste. Master cabinetmaker.

maître menuisier. Master joiner.

maîtrise. Mastership; freedom, of a corporation.

manchette. Armpad; also a padded crest rail, as the *manchette d'accoudoir sur le dossier* of a *voyeuse.*

manteau. Mantelshelf.

maquette. Model or rough sketch of a project.

marchand. Merchant, dealer, trader, shopkeeper.

marchepied. Step, bed step, pair of steps, footstool.

marque. Mark, stamp, brand.

marqueter. To inlay, to checker.

marqueterie. Marquetry, inlays of running or detached cursive patterns, floral arrangements, foliage, urns, utensils, landscapes, figures, and so on; also mosaic, geometric, or checkered patterns, as *marqueterie à cubes.* In English the latter forms may be distinguished as parquetry: an inlay of geometric patterns in wood. *Parqueterie* is equivalent to our use of "parquetry" for describing geometric patterns in flooring, and is not used in reference to general veneer work.

marqueteur. Marquetry worker.

marquise. Small seat or *canapé* for two, or smaller—as a wide easy chair. See *demi-canapé.*

mascaron. Mask, grotesque figure.

médaillier. Cabinet for a collection of medals.

menuiserie. Joinery, work of a joiner, a piece of joinery.

menuisier. Joiner.

menuisier-ébéniste. A craftsman qualified as a cabinetmaker as well as in the solid constructional work of the joiner.

menuisier-machiniste. Joiner-machinist.

mènuisier-sculpteur. A joiner also qualified as a wood carver. See *sculpteur en bois.*

menuisier-tourneur. Joiner-turner.

metropolitain, e. Of, pertaining to, or being a metropolis or principal city. Metropolis: the chief or capital city of a country, state, region, etc.; a principal seat or center (Webster). See *suburbain,* and *rustique.*

meuble. Piece of furniture.

meuble à perruques. Piece fashioned as a side table of commode plan with single, long, deep drawer to contain perukes.

meuble d'entredeux. Piece to be placed between two windows or doors, as a pier table or *table de trumeau,* or a case in the general form of a commode but fitted with a door or doors instead of drawers. Also applied to varying forms of the *desserte.* A low *meuble* with double doors (Lucotte).

meubles en-cas. See *en-cas.*

meuble serre-bijoux. Fitted jewel cabinet.

meubles régionaux. Regional furniture.

meubles rustique. Rustic, rude, unpolished, or rural furniture.

meubles usuels. Usual or ordinary furniture, as made for the bourgeoisie or wealthier citizens of Paris and other French cities.

miroir. Looking glass.

miroitier. Looking-glass maker.

montant, e. An upright member, stile, or post of a *meuble.*

moulure. Molding; *moulure en torsade:* cabled molding.

nacre. Mother-of-pearl.

ottomane. Ottoman; upholstered stool, seat, or couch without a back. Upholstered or caned settee of crescent shape, the sides curving inward at the seat front (Delafosse). A *canapé* with incurvate sides.

paille. Straw, as *siège de paille.*

panetière. Hanging or standing bread holder, livery cupboard; in Provence a piece composed mainly of turned spindles, in Burgundy often fitted with *grillage*.

panier. Basket, hamper.

paphose. Kidney-shaped settee with arched horseshoe back *en gondole* (Delafosse).

paravent. Screen, folding screen, multiple-fold screen, *paravent à six feuilles.*

parqueterie. See *marqueterie.*

patère. Patera, classic disklike ornament.

pavillon. Bed canopy of tentlike form; with flat-arched crest or with domed crowning (Roubo).

peint, e. Painted, as *meuble en bois peint.*

pelle-à-cul. Rural chair with shovel-form seat.

pendule. Clock, timepiece; generally used in reference to the smaller clocks, as a mantel clock, bracket clock with bracket, or table clock. Also *pendule à gaine* or *p. sur socle:* clock with matching pedestal-form support. Preferred by one authority for early types in contrast to *régulateur* for most tall clocks of later metropolitan workmanship. During the eighteenth century *pendule* and *horloge* were used interchangeably to describe both small and large clocks.

petit-pied. Small stand, as for flowers.

petite commode. A chest of drawers slightly smaller than the average commode (Roubo). A *commode à pieds* of small to medium size (Roubo).

pétrin. Kneading, or dough trough. See *maie* and *huche.*

piastres. Coins or coin motifs, as *rang de piastres:* row or band of imbricated coin motifs.

pièce de maîtrise. Acceptance piece made for submission to a group of jurors appointed by a *Communauté* in which a joiner or cabinetmaker sought admittance as a master.

pied de biche. Deer's foot, or a replica as used to terminate a cabriole leg.

pied en toupie. Top-shaped (or vase-shaped) foot.

piédestal. Pedestal, *gaine, socle.*

piédouche. A small pedestal or a console-form wall bracket for supporting a vase or bust.

pilastre. Pilaster, stile, or flat *montant* of a cabinet piece.

placage. Veneering.

plafond. Ceiling, ceiling painting, any overhead surface looked at from below; *plafonnage.*

plateau. Flat horizontal surface, as a table top or the marble slab of a commode.

pliant, e. Folding stool or chair; *table pliante:* folding table.

ployan. Folding X-stool (Delafosse).

poêle. Stove, furnace for warming a room—often of highly ornamental pedestal-form designs, as shown by Delafosse.

poignée. Handle or drawer pull, *main de tirage.*

poinçon. Punch or small stamp.

pointes d'asperge. Ornamental cable fillets, as in the flutings of *bronze doré* mounts used during the Louis XVI period.

pontil. A metal die used in impressing a craftsman's mark upon his completed work, generally held in a wood block with extending spur to be struck by a mallet or hammer.

porte. Door, cupboard door, as *armoire à deux portes;* ready.

porte-assiette. Plate stand.

porte-montre. Watch stand, in France, as well as Flanders and Germany; often finely carved and gilded or painted.

porte-musique. Music stand, canterbury.

postes. Greek wave band; Vitruvian scrolls.

postes feuillées. Foliated wave band.

poudreuse. Dressing table, *toilette* or *coiffeuse,* generally with enclosed side wells (*caissons*) and central lid with mirror inside; *table de toilette* (Lucotte).

poudreuse-table d'accouchée. See *table de malade.*

presse à lin. Linen press or cupboard.

prie-Dieu. Chair or other *meuble* for kneeling at prayers.

privilégié du Roi. A distinction associated with special advantages awarded by the King to favored craftsmen, indicated by this legend or the use of *fleurs de lis* in their *pontil* marks.

province. An administrative district; country. *Vivre en province:* to live in the country—not in a city or large town of a province. See *régional.*

Provinces (French. For administrative purposes, France, previous to the Revolution of 1789–1799, was divided into the thirty-three provinces listed below. Leading furniture centers located in the majority of these provinces are noted where populations totaled 20,000 or more at the close of the eighteenth century, when the entire population of the country was 26,000,000, and that of Paris was 680,000.

ALSACE. Strasbourg (43,064).
ANJOU. Angers (30,000).
ARTOIS.
AUNIS.
AUVERGNE.
BÉARN.
BERRY.
BOURBONNAIS.
BOURGOGNE. Dijon (20,000).
BRETAGNE. Nantes (58,000), Bennes (35,000), Brest (30,000).
CHAMPAGNE. Troyes (32,000).
COMTAT VENAISSIN. Avignon (26,000).
DAUPHINÉ. Grenoble (24,000).
FLANDRE. Lille (67,000).
FOIX.
FRANCHE-COMTÉ. Besançon (25,500).

GASCOGNE.
GUYENNE. Bordeaux (84,000).
ÎLE-DE-FRANCE. Paris (680,000), Versailles (80,000).
LANGUEDOC. Toulouse (56,000), Montpellier (30,000).
LIMOUSIN.
LORRAINE. Metz (40,000), Nancy (32,000).
LYONNAIS. Lyon (115,000).
MAINE.
NIVERNAIS.
NORMANDIE. Rouen (72,500), Caen (32,000).
ORLÉANAIS. Orléans (39,500), Angers (30,000), Bourges (25,000), Tours (21,600).
PICARDIE. Amiens (43,500), Abbeville (20,000).
POITOU.
PROVENCE. Marseille (87,410), Toulon (28,000), Aix (24,000).
ROUSSILLON.
SAINTON ET ANGOUMOIS.
TOURAINE.

provincial, e. Provincial, country-like, countrified. See *rustique.*

pupitre. Desk, table-desk.

pupitre à crémaillère. Table for drawing, with rising top supported by ratchet stays; *table à tronchin.*

pupitre à musique. Stand with music desk.

quenouille. Bedpost, *colonne, pilier.*

rafraîchissoir. Wine cooler.

rallonge. Leaf of a telescopic table.

rang de perles. Row or band of pearl ornament.

rang de piastres. See *piastres.*

régional, e. Of a region, of a district; district. *Meubles régionaux:* furniture of various regions or districts.

régulateur. Generally used in connection with French tall-case clocks produced by metropolitan makers during the eighteenth century, this term is allied to the English "regulator": a standard clock used for timing other clocks, usually fitted with a dead-beat escapement, and often kept as a fixture in a clockmaker's shop.

rideau. Curtain; screen. *Rideau de lit:* bed curtain. *Secrétaire à rideaux:* writing table or cabinet with tambour shutters.

rinceau. Classic running and branching foliage ornament, as in *bronze doré* frieze appliqués of the Louis XVI period (and in sixteenth-century carving).

rocaille. Pebbles, rockwork, shellwork, grottowork.

rocailleux, euse. Pebbly, stony.

rouet. Spinning wheel.

roulette. Caster, small wheel, roller.

ruban. Ribbon, stripe. *Ruban enroulé:* rolled, scrolled, or spiraled ribbon or band.

rural, e. See *rustique.*

rustique. Rustic, rural, coarse, rough, rude, unpolished.

sablier. Hourglass, sandglass.

sabot. Shoe, socket at the base of a straight leg. Sometimes used in reference to applied toe mounts with no lower cuppings or sockets; see *chausson. Sabot en patte de lion:* toe capping with socket, the outer modeling in the form of a lion's paw.

salière. Salt holder, saltcellar.

sculpteur en bois. Wood carver, often a specializing craftsman or artist employed by the *menuisier.*

secrétaire. Secretary, writing desk, or bureau.

secrétaire à abattant. See *abattant. Secrétaire en armoire*—with falling *tablette* (Lucotte).

secrétaire à archives. Cabinet with *cartonniers* contained in an upper open-front section (Lalonde).

secrétaire à panse. Cylinder-front desk, *bureau à cylindre.*

secrétaire-bibliothèque. Desk with upper cabinet or cupboard section.

secrétaire-chiffonnier. Tall chest of drawers containing a writing section.

secrétaire-commode. Chest of drawers with writing section; *commode-secrétaire.*

secrétaire en tombeau. Desk with slant-front writing section, generally used in reference to a *bureau à dos d'âne.*

semainier. Tall chest of seven drawers.

serre-bijoux. Jewel case, small jewel coffer or cabinet on table stand.

serre-papiers. Paper holder; open-faced cabinet with compartments for papers. Nest of pigeonholes (Lucotte).

servante. Dumb-waiter (*serviteur fidèle*); portable serving stand or table, side table for serving; sometimes used in reference to a *desserte.*

serviteur muet. Dumb-waiter.

siège. Seat, chair, bench.

siège à l'antique. Chair of Greek or Roman form.

siège à la capucine. Chair with rush or straw seat.

siège d'affaires. See *chaise percée.*

siège d'aisances. See *bidet.*

siège de paille. Chair with straw seat.

singerie. A composition incorporating one or more figures of monkeys; monkey antic.

sofa. Sofa-bed or couch; some forms of the *lit à la turque* and the *ottomane* are referred to as *sofas.* Ample *canapé* of usual form, with open arms (Delafosse). *Canapé* with back curving into conforming upholstered sides *en gondole* (Lucotte).

suburbain, e. Of, pertaining to, or located in the suburbs. (Suburb: An outlying part of a city or town; a smaller place adjacent to a city);

U.S. Blending or characterized by the blending of the urban and rural (Webster).

syndic. Syndic, agent.

table à bijoux. Table for keeping jewelry.

table à coiffeuse. Dressing table. See *poudreuse.*

table à culbute. Table with somersaulting section. See *table volante.*

table à déjeuner. Breakfast or luncheon table, sometimes a *guéridon* or *table-guéridon* with marble top.

table à écran. Table fitted with a screen panel.

table à écrire. Writing table.

table à feu. Fireside table or stand.

table à fleurs. Table with well or wells for plants or stem flowers; *jardinière.*

table à gradin. Table with recessed superstructure, as a *bonheur du jour* or larger writing table with shallow cabinet section.

table à jeu. Gaming table; *table de jeu.*

table à jeu pliant. Gaming table with folding top.

table à l'antique. Table of Greek or Roman form.

table à manger. Dining-room table.

table à rallonge. Telescopic table.

table à rideau. Table with recess enclosed by a panel or tambour shutter.

table à rognon. Kidney-shaped table.

table à tambour. Table with tambour cupboard.

table à tirettes. Table with recesses enclosed by sliding panels.

table à trictrac. Backgammon table.

table à tronchin. Drawing or architect's table, with raised top.

table à volets. Table with lateral drop leaves.

table ambulante. Easily portable table or stand.

table-bouillotte. Circular card table with marble top, two small drawers, and two pull-out slides; generally with round tapering legs.

table-bureau. Writing table with flat top; see *bureau plat.*

table d'accouchée. See *table de malade.*

table de cabaret. Table for tea, coffee, or other drinking service.

table de chevet. Table used at the head of a bedstead.

table de cuisine. Kitchen table; many types (with various alterations) now appearing in American living rooms as center tables, writing tables, and so on.

table de dame. Any of the lighter and more delicately treated tables made for use by ladies.

table de lit. Bedside table.

table de malade. Table with separate top section removable as a tray with short sectional legs; *table d'accouchée.*

table de milieu. Center table.

table de nuit. Night or bedside table, or stand.

table de toilette. Dressing table (Lucotte).

table de trumeau. Pier table; often applied to oblong tables, or to the usual (shaped) console forms with an open shelf or shelves, as a *console-desserte.*

table en haricot. Table with kidney-bean shaping; *table à rognon.*

table extensible. Table with folding top or drawer leaves.

table-guéridon. Circular table of medium or large size; see *guéridon.*

table liseuse. Reading table.

table ouvrante. Table with opening top or leaves.

table pliant. Table with drop leaves, or folding leaves.

table-vitrine. Display table with frieze well revealed through a glass panel or panels.

table volante. Portable table or stand, as a *servante.* A *table à culbute.* A *secrétaire mobile:* with hinged quadrantal section of pigeonholes rising from beneath the frieze (Roubo).

tablette. Shelf, tablet, small table; an *abattant* (Lucotte).

tabletterie. Inlaid work.

tablier. Apron of a table or chair.

tabouret. Stool, small stand in the form of a wood stool.

tamisadou. Flour cupboard somewhat similar to a *buffet bas,* made to hold the cylindrical flour sifter; popular in Provence.

tête-à-tête. Small *canapé* for two persons partially facing in conversation.

tire-main. Drawer handle or pull.

tirette. Sliding panel in front of a recess or cupboard, generally operating sideways—as in the *buffet à glissants* of Provence.

tiroir. Drawer.

tiroirs sans traverse apparente. A structural method of French and other Continental cabinetmakers, in which the traverse rails, separating and supporting the drawers of commodes and other case pieces, are largely concealed behind the extended facings of the drawers.

toilette. Dressing table; *poudreuse, coiffeuse.*

torchère. Candelabrum; stand to hold a candelabrum.

tore de lauriers. Torus molding enriched with laurel leaves.

tourneur. Turner.

travailleuse. Worktable or stand.

traversin. Bolster.

tricoteuse. Knitting table.

trictrac. Backgammon.

trou-madame. Pigeonhole; the game of bagatelle.

trumeau. Pier, pier mirror; section of wall paneling with mirror, often surmounted by a painting.

truquage. Faking.

truqueur. Faker.

turquoise. Daybed with outcurving *dossiers* at either end, the terminals of the *montants* voluted; *sofa* with similarly shaped end *dossiers* but with an upholstered back: *turquoise à trois chevets. Canapé* of oval plan with arched horseshoe back curving down to the front seat rail (Delafosse).

vaisselier. Open-shelf cabinet or dresser, for plates, in one section or with cupboard below; the *vaisselier-égouttoir* of Breton.

vantail. Folding door, or one of the leaves.

veilleuse. Night light. Columnar pedestal with oval or square crest for holding small articles, a candle light at the rear shielded by an oval screen panel (Delafosse).

veilleuse. *Canapé* or daybed with seat of either violin or kidney shape, the curved back rising at one end with the side deeply returned above the front seat rail—sometimes also called a *grand canapé en gondole.* Boat-shaped *canapé* with deeply incurvate sides (Roubo); a similar form shown by Lucotte as a *sofa* or *chaise longue.* A daybed of serpentine form with single low *dossier* (Lucotte).

veilleuse en forme d'ottomane. Canapé with pronounced horseshoe shaping, one end with slightly raised back curve (Delafosse).

vernis Martin. A varnish finish employed by Guillaume, Simon-Étienne, and Robert Martin, on furniture, musical instruments, wall paneling, coaches, sedan chairs, and sledges; especially famous for the green tone they achieved. Their plain grounds were often flecked with gold; decorations were carried out in floral ornament, figures, coats of arms, and so forth.

verrier. Hanging or standing shelves for glasses.

vide-poche. Pouchlike space, such as a pocket let into the arm of an easy chair, to hold personal articles.

vitrine. Display case.

voyeuse. Conversation or straddle chair with shaped seat narrowing toward the back, generally surmounted by a padded crest rail, or *accoudoir à manchette;* with crest rolled backward (Radel).

PARISIAN FURNITURE

Right:

LOUIS XV CARVED BEECHWOOD CHAISE À LA REINE,
Michel Cresson (r. m. 1740), circa 1745–1750.

Below right:

LOUIS XV CARVED AND GILDED FAUTEUIL À LA REINE, circa 1750. Courtesy of French & Company, Inc., New York City.

Below:

LOUIS XV CARVED AND GILDED FAUTEUIL À LA REINE,
Nicholas Heurtaut (r. m. 1755), circa 1755–1760.

Right:

LOUIS XV CARVED BEECHWOOD BERGÈRE, circa 1755–1765.
Courtesy of French & Company, Inc., New York City.

Below:

LOUIS XV CARVED AND PAINTED BERGÈRE, circa 1755–1765.

Below right:

LOUIS XV CARVED BEECHWOOD BERGÈRE, circa 1750–1760.

LOUIS XV CARVED BEECHWOOD CANAPÈ, circa 1755–1765.
Courtesy of French & Company, Inc., New York City.

LOUIS XV CARVED BEECHWOOD DUCHESSE À BATEAU, circa 1750–1760.

LOUIS XV PAINTED CHAISE À DOSSIER CROSSÉ, circa 1765.

LOUIS XV PAINTED BERGÈRE, circa 1765–1770.

LOUIS XV CARVED AND GILDED FAUTEUIL À LA REINE, circa 1765–1770.

LOUIS XV CARVED AND GILDED FAUTEUIL À LA REINE, circa 1765–1770.

LOUIS XV AMARANTH AND TULIPWOOD MARQUETRY TABLE AMBULANTE, circa 1770–1775.

LOUIS XV INLAID TULIPWOOD TABLE DE MILIEU, circa 1770–1775.

LOUIS XV TULIPWOOD AND DECORATED BLACK LACQUER TABLE DE MILIEU, circa 1770–1775.

LOUIS XV TULIPWOOD AND VIOLET WOOD MARQUETRY TABLE LISEUSE, circa 1767–1775.
Courtesy of Jacques & Henri Barroux, Paris.

LOUIS XV TULIPWOOD AND AMARANTH MARQUETRY BUREAU À PENTE,
Adrien Faizelot Delorme (r. m. 1748), circa 1765.

LOUIS XV DECORATED BLACK LACQUER
PETIT BUREAU DE DAME, circa 1765.

LOUIS XV DECORATED BLACK LACQUER
SECRÉTAIRE EN TOMBEAU, circa 1765.

LOUIS XV EBONY BUREAU PLAT MOUNTED IN BRONZE DORÉ,
Style of Charles Cressent (w. 1714–1757), circa 1735.
Collection of Alan P. Good, Esq., Glympton Park, Oxfordshire.
Courtesy of Morton Lee, London.

LOUIS XV INLAID VIOLET WOOD BUREAU PLAT,
Adrien Faizelot Delorme (r. m. 1748), circa 1755.
Courtesy of French & Company, Inc., New York City.

LOUIS XV INLAID VIOLET WOOD AND TULIPWOOD BUREAU PLAT, circa 1760.

LOUIS XV INLAID TULIPWOOD BUREAU PLAT, circa 1765.
Courtesy of Jacques & Henri Barroux, Paris.

LOUIS XV TULIPWOOD MARQUETRY COMMODE,
B. Péridiez (w. c. 1750-1757), circa 1750.
Courtesy of French & Company, Inc., New York City.

LOUIS XV INLAID MAHOGANY AND AMARANTH COMMODE, circa 1745.
Courtesy of the Rijksmuseum, Amsterdam.

LOUIS XV VIOLET WOOD AND TULIPWOOD MARQUETRY COMMODE, circa 1760.
Courtesy of Jacques & Henri Barroux, Paris.

LOUIS XV AMARANTH AND MARQUETRY COMMODE,
Jean-Pierre Latz (w. c. 1740–1754), circa 1750–1754.
Courtesy of French & Company, Inc., New York City.

LOUIS XV TULIPWOOD AND DECORATED BLACK LACQUER COMMODE, circa 1765.
Courtesy of Jacques & Henri Barroux, Paris.

LOUIS XV TULIPWOOD MARQUETRY COMMODE, circa 1770.
Joseph Schmitz (r. m. 1761).

LOUIS XVI CARVED AND GILDED VOYEUSE, circa 1775.
The form designated by Delafosse as a *Flamande*.

LOUIS XVI CARVED, PAINTED, AND GILDED
FAUTEUIL EN CABRIOLET.
Jean-René Nadal (r. m. 1756), circa 1775.
Courtesy of French & Company, Inc., New York City.

LOUIS XVI CARVED AND GILDED CANAPÉ, Adrien-Pierre Dupain (r. m. 1772), circa 1780.
Courtesy of French & Company, Inc., New York City.

LOUIS XVI CARVED AND GILDED CANAPÉ, Claude Chevigny (r. m. 1768), circa 1785.
Courtesy of French & Company, Inc., New York City.

LOUIS XVI CARVED AND PAINTED
CHAISE EN CABRIOLET, circa 1785.

LOUIS XVI CARVED AND GILDED
CHAISE EN CABRIOLET, circa 1785.
Paul-François Jean (r. m. 1784).

LOUIS XVI CARVED MAHOGANY
FAUTEUIL DE BUREAU, circa 1780–1785.
Courtesy of Monsieur Gaston Bensimon,
New York City.

LOUIS XVI CARVED BEECHWOOD
FAUTEUIL DE BUREAU, circa 1780–1785.

LOUIS XVI CARVED AND PAINTED BERGÈRE, circa 1785.

LOUIS XVI CARVED AND PAINTED FAUTEUIL,
Adrien-Pierre Dupain, (r. m. 1772), circa 1785–1790.

LOUIS XVI CARVED AND PAINTED CANAPÉ,
Adrien-Pierre Dupain, (r. m. 1772), circa 1785–1790.

LOUIS XVI CARVED AND GILDED FAUTEUIL, circa 1790.
Style of Georges Jacob, and of his imitator, Henri Jacob.

LOUIS XVI CARVED AND GILDED BERGÈRE, circa 1790.
Style of Georges Jacob, and of his imitator, Henri Jacob.

LOUIS XVI CARVED AND GILDED CANAPÉ, circa 1790.
Style of Georges Jacob, and of his imitator, Henri Jacob.

Above left:

LOUIS XVI INLAID TULIPWOOD TABLE AMBULANTE,
Charles Topino (r. m. 1773), circa 1775.

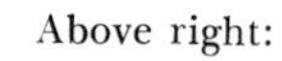

Above right:

LOUIS XVI INLAID TULIPWOOD TABLE AMBULANTE, circa 1775.

Left:

LOUIS XVI INLAID TULIPWOOD PETITE TABLE À ÉCRIRE,
circa 1775.

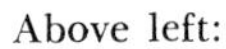

Above left:

LOUIS XVI TULIPWOOD AND MARQUETRY TABLE AMBULANTE, circa 1775. Style of Léonard Boudin, Pierre Roussel, and Charles Topino. Courtesy of French & Company, Inc., New York City.

Above right:

LOUIS XVI TULIPWOOD AND CITRONNIER MARQUETRY TABLE AMBULANTE, attributed to Roger Vandercruse, known as *Lacroix* (r. m. 1755) , circa 1775.

Right:

LOUIS XVI TULIPWOOD AND MARQUETRY TABLE À GRADIN, attributed to Léonard Boudin (r. m. 1761) , circa 1775. Courtesy of French & Company, Inc., New York City.

LOUIS XVI TULIPWOOD AND AMARANTH MARQUETRY BONHEUR DU JOUR,
Pierre Denizot (r. m. 1740), circa 1780.
Courtesy of French & Company, Inc., New York City.

LOUIS XVI TULIPWOOD AND MARQUETRY BONHEUR DU JOUR,
Charles Topino (r. m. 1773), circa 1780–1785.
Courtesy of French & Company, Inc., New York City.

LOUIS XVI TULIPWOOD BONHEUR DU JOUR, circa 1785–1790.

LOUIS XVI MAHOGANY BUREAU À CYLINDRE,
François-Ignace Papst (r. m. 1785), circa 1785–1790.

LOUIS XVI INLAID TULIPWOOD BUREAU PLAT AND MEUBLE AVEC CARTONNIER,
The cartonnier section signed by Pierre Bonnemain, (r. m. 1751), circa 1785–1795,
and bearing the label of the Château de Fontainebleau.
Courtesy of French & Company, Inc., New York City.

LOUIS XVI TULIPWOOD AND MARQUETRY COMMODE, circa 1773–1782.
With *pontil* marks of Charles Topino and Louis-Noël Malle.

LOUIS XVI INLAID TULIPWOOD COMMODE,
Claude-Charles Saunier (r. m. 1752), circa 1775–1780.
Courtesy of French & Company, Inc., New York City.

LOUIS XVI INLAID TULIPWOOD COMMODE,
Jean-Chrysostôme Stumpff (r. m. 1766), circa 1780–1785.

LOUIS XVI INLAID AMARANTH AND SYCAMORE
MEUBLE D'ENTREDEUX, circa 1790.

LOUIS XVI MAHOGANY COMMODE, circa 1790.

LOUIS XVI MAHOGANY COMMODE, circa 1790–1795.

LOUIS XVI KINGWOOD AND MARQUETRY SECRÉTAIRE DE DAME, circa 1780–1785.

LOUIS XVI RUBY WOOD AND MARQUETRY SECRÉTAIRE À ABATTANT,
Jean-Henri Riesener (r. m. 1768), circa 1785.

METROPOLITAN FURNITURE OF PROVINCES OTHER THAN ÎLE DE FRANCE

LE CHAMBRE DU ROI, CHÂTEAU DE ROHAN, STRASBOURG, PROVINCE OF ALSACE, Strasbourg, 1735–1740. Occupied by Louis XV in 1744, and by Marie-Antoinette in 1770. Courtesy of the Musée du Château de Rohan, Strasbourg.

LOUIS XV CARVED, PAINTED, AND PARCEL-GILDED BOISERIE, FROM THE PROVINCE OF NORMANDIE, Rouen, circa 1745–1755.
With matching carved and gilded console.
Courtesy of the Röhsska Konstslöjdmuseet, Göteborg.

Above left:

LOUIS XV CARVED FRUITWOOD FAUTEUIL CANNÉ, circa 1740–1750.

Above right:

LOUIS XV CARVED WALNUT FAUTEUIL, circa 1740–1750.
Courtesy of French & Company, Inc., New York City.

Right:

LOUIS XV CARVED WALNUT BERGÈRE À OREILLES, circa 1735–1745.

LOUIS XV CARVED BEECHWOOD FAUTEUIL CANNÉ, circa 1745–1755.

LOUIS XV CARVED BEECHWOOD FAUTEUIL CANNÉ, circa 1745–1755. Stamped with the initials H L B.

LOUIS XV CARVED WALNUT CANAPÉ À JOUES, circa 1735–1745.
Courtesy of French & Company, Inc., New York City.

LOUIS XV CARVED BEECHWOOD FAUTEUIL CANNÉ, circa 1745–1755. Fraudulently stamped with a mark purporting to be that of Jean-Baptiste Gourdin.

LOUIS XV CARVED BEECHWOOD CHAISE, circa 1750.

LOUIS XV CARVED WALNUT FAUTEUIL À LA REINE, circa 1750–1760.

LOUIS XV CARVED BEECHWOOD FAUTEUIL À LA REINE, circa 1750–1760.

LOUIS XV CARVED BEECHWOOD FAUTEUIL CANNÉ,
Pierre Nogaret, Lyon, circa 1755–1765.
Courtesy of the Musée des Arts décoratifs, Paris.

LOUIS XV CARVED AND PAINTED FAUTEUIL CANNÉ.
One of a set of fourteen. Pierre Nogaret, Lyon, circa 1755–1765.
Courtesy of the Musée Nissim de Camondo, Paris

LOUIS XV CARVED AND PAINTED CANAPÉ,
Pierre Nogaret, Lyon, circa 1755–1765.
Courtesy of the Musée Nissim de Camando, Paris.

LOUIS XV CARVED BEECHWOOD CHAISE CANNÉ,
Pierre Nogaret, Lyon, circa 1760–1770.
Courtesy of the Musée Historique de Lyon.

LOUIS XV CARVED BEECHWOOD FAUTEUIL CANNÉ,
François Canot, Lyon, circa 1755-1770.
Courtesy of the Musée Lyonnais des Arts décoratifs.

LOUIS XV CARVED WALNUT CHAISE
À LA REINE, Lyon, circa 1760–1770.

LOUIS XV CARVED WALNUT CHAISE CANNÉ.
Pierre Nogaret, Lyon, circa 1755–1765.
Courtesy of the Musée Historique de Lyon.

Above left:

LOUIS XV CARVED WALNUT CHAISE, circa 1745–1760.
Courtesy of the Musée et Bibliothèque Calvet, Avignon.

Above: right:

LOUIS XV CARVED WALNUT FAUTEUIL, circa 1750–1765.
Courtesy of the Musée et Bibliothèque Calvet, Avignon.

Left:

LOUIS XV CARVED BEECHWOOD BERGÈRE À JOUES,
circa 1735–1745.

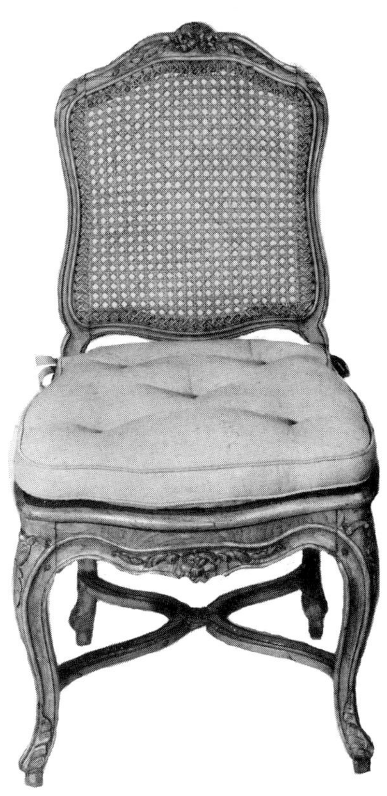

LOUIS XV CARVED BEECHWOOD CHAISE CANNÉ, circa 1755–1765. Stamped CHELANT, attributed to Lyon.

LOUIS XV CARVED BEECHWOOD FAUTEUIL CANNÉ, François Canot, Lyon, circa 1755–1765. Courtesy of the Musée Historique de Lyon.

LOUIS XV CARVED WALNUT CHAISE CANNÉ, Pierre Nogaret, Lyon, circa 1755–1765. Courtesy of the Musée Historique de Lyon.

LOUIS XV CARVED BEECHWOOD CHAISE CANNÉ, François Canot, Lyon, circa 1755–1765. Courtesy of the Musée Historique de Lyon.

LOUIS XV CARVED WALNUT FAUTEUIL À LA REINE, circa 1755-1765. Courtesy of the Musée et Bibliothèque Calvet, Avignon.

LOUIS XV CARVED BEECHWOOD FAUTEUIL À LA REINE, Lyon, circa 1755–1765. Fraudulently stamped with a mark purporting to be that of Pierre Falconet.

LOUIS XV CARVED WOOD AND GESSO FAUTEUIL À LA REINE, Lyon, circa 1755–1765.

LOUIS XV CARVED AND PAINTED FAUTEUIL À LA REINE, circa 1760–1770. Stamped N C FOURNIER.

LOUIS CARVED WALNUT CANAPÉ, circa 1755–1765.
Courtesy of the Musée et Bibliothèque Calvet, Avignon.

LOUIS XV CARVED WALNUT CANAPÉ,
Pierre Nogaret, Lyon, circa 1755–1765.

Left:

LOUIS XV CARVED BEECHWOOD FAUTEUIL À LA REINE,
circa 1755–1765.

Below left:

LOUIS XV CARVED AND PAINTED FAUTEUIL EN CABRIOLET,
circa 1760–1770. Courtesy of the Musée Nissim de Camondo, Paris.

Below right:

LOUIS XV CARVED BEECHWOOD FAUTEUIL EN CABRIOLET,
Pierre Nogaret, Lyon, circa 1770.

Above left:

LOUIS XV CARVED AND PAINTED FAUTEUIL EN CABRIOLET, circa 1765–1775. Courtesy of the Musea Van Oudheden, Antwerp.

Above right:

LOUIS XV CARVED WALNUT CHAISE EN CABRIOLET, circa 1765–1775. Stamped BLEROUGE.

Right:

LOUIS XV CARVED BEECHWOOD FAUTEUIL EN CABRIOLET, circa 1765–1775. Courtesy of the Musée et Bibliothèque Calvet, Avignon.

LOUIS XV CARVED AND PAINTED PETITE VEILLEUSE, circa 1755–1765.
Courtesy of French & Company, Inc., New York City.

LOUIS XV CARVED AND PAINTED OTTOMANE, circa 1755–1765.

LOUIS XV CARVED AND PAINTED CHAISE CANNÉ,
Pierre Nogaret, Lyon, circa 1755–1765.
Courtesy of the Musée des Arts décoratifs, Paris.

LOUIS XV CARVED AND PAINTED
FAUTEUIL CANNÉ, Lyon, circa 1755–1765.

LOUIS XV CARVED WALNUT CANAPÉ,
circa 1755–1765. Stamped with the initials R Y.
Courtesy of Frederick P. Victoria, New York City.

LOUIS XV CARVED WALNUT FAUTEUIL EN CABRIOLET, circa 1760–1770.

LOUIS XV CARVED AND PAINTED FAUTEUIL EN CABRIOLET, circa 1765–1775.

LOUIS XV-XVI CARVED WALNUT AND BEECH FAUTEUIL À LA REINE, circa 1770–1780.

LOUIS XV-XVI CARVED WALNUT FAUTEUIL À LA REINE, circa 1770–1780.

LOUIS XV-XVI CARVED AND PAINTED LIT À LA POLONAISE, circa 1770–1780.
Shown without the *couronne* and its supports.
Courtesy of French & Company, Inc., New York City.

LOUIS XV BURL ASH AND MARQUETRY BUREAU GALBÉ.
Pierre or Jean-François Hache, Grenoble, circa 1765–1775.

LOUIS XV-XVI INLAID WALNUT BUREAU À PENTE, circa 1770–1780.

LOUIS XIV CARVED AND GILDED TABLE-CONSOLE, early 18th Century.
Courtesy of the Musée et Bibliothèque Calvet, Avignon.

LOUIS XV CARVED AND GILDED CONSOLE, circa 1735–1745.

LOUIS XV CARVED OAK CONSOLE, circa 1735–1745.
Reflecting the influence of Bernard Toro.

LOUIS XV CARVED AND GILDED CONSOLE, circa 1750–1760.
Courtesy of Monsieur Gaston Bensimon, New York City.

LOUIS XV CARVED AND GILDED CONSOLE, Provence, circa 1745–1755.
Reflecting the influence of Bernard Toro.

LOUIS XV CARVED AND GILDED CONSOLE, circa 1745–1755.
Courtesy of Monsieur Gaston Bensimon, New York City.

LOUIS XV CARVED AND GILDED CONSOLE, circa 1750–1760.
Courtesy of Monsieur Gaston Bensimon, New York City.

LOUIS XV CARVED OAK CONSOLE, circa 1750–1760.

LOUIS XV CARVED AND GILDED CONSOLE, circa 1755–1765.

LOUIS XV CARVED, PAINTED AND GILDED CONSOLE, circa 1760–1770.

LOUIS XV INLAID PALISANDER COMMODE, circa 1735–1750.

LOUIS XV INLAID WALNUT COMMODE, circa 1735–1750.

LOUIS XV INLAID PALISANDER COMMODE À LA RÉGENCE, circa 1735–1750.

LOUIS XV INLAID PALISANDER COMMODE À LA RÉGENCE, circa 1735–1750.
With mark purporting to be that of Mathieu Criaerd.

LOUIS XV INLAID KINGWOOD COMMODE À LA RÉGENCE, circa 1740–1750.
Courtesy of the Musée et Bibliothèque Calvet, Avignon.

LOUIS XV INLAID KINGWOOD COMMODE, circa 1755–1765.

LOUIS XV INLAID KINGWOOD AND TULIPWOOD COMMODE, circa 1760–1765.

LOUIS XV INLAID KINGWOOD AND TULIPWOOD COMMODE, circa 1760–1765.

LOUIS XV INLAID KINGWOOD COMMODE, circa 1750–1765.

LOUIS XV INLAID KINGWOOD AND TULIPWOOD COMMODE, circa 1755–1765.

LOUIS XV INLAID PALISANDER COMMODE, circa 1745–1755.

LOUIS XV INLAID PALISANDER COMMODE, circa 1750–1760.

LOUIS XV INLAID KINGWOOD AND TULIPWOOD COMMODE, circa 1765–1775.
Stamped BOUDIN, with no initial, but with JME mark.

LOUIS XV INLAID KINGWOOD AND TULIPWOOD COMMODE, circa 1765–1775.

LOUIS XV INLAID KINGWOOD COMMODE, circa 1765–1775.

LOUIS XV INLAID TULIPWOOD COMMODE, circa 1770–1780.

LOUIS XV AMARANTH MARQUETRY COMMODE, circa 1765–1770.
With mark purporting to be that of François Rübestück.

LOUIS XV AMARANTH AND TULIPWOOD MARQUETRY COMMODE,
Grenoble, circa 1775.

LOUIS XV KINGWOOD AND TULIPWOOD MARQUETRY COMMODE, circa 1765–1770. Courtesy of French & Company, Inc., New York City.

LOUIS XV KINGWOOD AND TULIPWOOD MARQUETRY COMMODE, circa 1765–1775. Apparently made by a German *ébéniste,* possibly working outside of Paris or in the suburb of Saint-Antoine.

BIBLIOTHÈQUE IN THE CHÂTEAU DE ROHAN, Bernard Cocke, Strasbourg, 1741.
Courtesy of the Musées Municipaux, Strasbourg.

LOUIS XV BURL ASH AND MARQUETRY SECRÉTAIRE À ABATTANT,
Jean-François Hache, Grenoble, circa 1770–1775.
Courtesy of the Musée Lyonnais des Arts décoratifs.

A GRE[illegible]OBLE.

HACHE Fils, Ébéniſte de Monſeigne[illegible] DUC D'ORLEANS, vend & fait en ébéniſterie d'un genre nouveau[illegible] unique, en bois des Indes & autres de pays, louppes & racines teintes de diverſes [illegible]aleurs, avec des fleurs & marqueteries, toute ſorte de Bureaux, Commodes, Secretaires, Bibliothéques, Serre-papiers, Encoignures & Coins de cheminée, Tablettes pour mettre des livres, Tables de jeu, Tables de quadrille pliantes, Tables en mouchoir, Tables à trictrac, Tables pour écrire & manger dans le lit, Tables en ſecretaire, Tables en colimaçon, Tables à deſſus de marbre pour mettre ſous des trumeaux avec tiroirs & une tablette qui ſe tire pour écrire; & généralement toute ſorte de Tables.

Secretaires en armoire, Secretaires à culbutte, Secretaires de campagne plians, Secretaires en encoignure, Trictracs & Damiers de tous prix, Bidets de toute eſpece avec des ſeringues, Bidets à doſſiers, Bidets en tabouret, Bidets de campagne plians, Chaiſes percées de toute façon, Chaiſes de commodité figurant trois tomes d'hiſtoire, & d'autres figurant un livre; toute ſorte d'Ecrans & Pupitres, Porte-Miſſel, Pupitres à la Mahon. Chandeliers à cremalliere, Coffres-forts à ſecret, Magaſin à tabac, Caſſettes, Néceſſaires, Quarrés de toilette, Moulins à caffé, Boëte de pendule, Coffre en cuiſiniere, Chaiſes pliantes en bâton, Tables de nuit, Vuide-poches, Chiffonnieres, Bureaux de toilette, Cabarets, Ecritoires de toute façon; & généralement toute ſorte d'ouvrages d'ébéniſterie.

Il fait auſſi Chaiſes, Fauteuils, Sophas, Canapés, Ducheſſes, Perroquets, Chambranles de cheminées, Buffets avec ſculpture, Parquets, Fougeres, Lambris, Portes, Croiſées, Armoires, Commodes, Secretaires & Tables en noyer. En un mot tous les ouvrages ci-deſſus en menuiſerie, le tout du dernier goût & à juſte prix.

Il vend auſſi des Tables & Cheminées de marbre, de Suiſſe, France, Italie, *&c.*

ETIQUETTE AFFIXED TO THE INTERIOR OF THE HACHE SECRÉTAIRE.
Courtesy of the Musée Lyonnais des Arts décoratifs.

LOUIS XV INLAID KINGWOOD AND
TULIPWOOD SEMAINIER, circa 1765–1775.

LOUIS XV INLAID KINGWOOD AND TULIPWOOD
SECRÉTAIRE À ABATTANT, circa 1765–1775.
Courtesy of the Musée et Bibliothèque Calvet, Avignon.

.OUIS XV TULIPWOOD AND MARQUETRY CABINET À RIDEAUX,
French or Rhenish, circa 1765–1775.
Courtesy of H. Blairman & Sons Ltd., London.

LOUIS XV AMARANTH AND TULIPWOOD MARQUETRY
SECRÉTAIRE À ABATTANT, circa 1765–1775.
With fraudulent mark purporting to be that of Charles Chevallier.

EARLY LOUIS XV TRUMEAU WITH OIL PAINTING, AND A CONSOLE
IN THE MANNER OF BERNARD TORO (1672–1731).
Courtesy of the Musée et Bibliothèque Calvet, Avignon.

LOUIS XV CHEMINÉE WITH CARVED AND GILDED CADRE AND MARBLE CHAMBRANLE, Rouen, circa 1735–1745.
Courtesy of French & Company, Inc., New York City.

LOUIS XV CARVED AND GILDED PIER MIRROR, circa 1745–1755.

LOUIS XV TRUMEAU WITH CARVED AND GILDED CADRE, circa 1745–1755.

CARVED AND GILDED WALL MIRROR IN THE RÉGENCE TASTE, early 18th Century.
Courtesy of the Musée et Bibliothèque Calvet, Avignon.

LOUIS XV CARVED AND GILDED WALL MIRROR, circa 1745–1755. Courtesy of Frederick P. Victoria, New York City.

LOUIS XV CARVED AND GILDED WALL MIRROR, circa 1750–1760.
Courtesy of the Musée et Bibliothèque Calvet, Avignon.

LOUIS XV CARVED AND GILDED WALL MIRROR, circa 1755–1765
Courtesy of Frederick P. Victoria, New York City.

LOUIS XV MARQUETRY ÉTAGÈRE D'ANGLE, circa 1770-1775.
Jean-François Hache, Grenoble,
Courtesy of the Musée Nissim de Camondo, Paris.

LOUIS XV CARVED AND GILDED PIER MIRROR, circa 1760–1770.

LOUIS XV PENDULE D'APPLIQUE, IN GREEN-TINTED HORN AND BRONZE DORÉ, circa 1750–1760.
The dial plate inscribed COUTTEREZ À LYON.
Courtesy of the Musée Lyonnais des Arts décoratifs.

GRAND SALON OF THE CHÂTEAU BORÉLY. MARSEILLE, PROVINCE OF PROVENCE, circa 1780.
Courtesy of the Musée d'Archéologie de Marseille.

LOUIS XVI CARVED AND PAINTED FAUTEUIL À LA REINE, circa 1775.
Collection of the Comte de Rancourt, Orléans.

LOUIS XVI CARVED AND PAINTED BERGÈRE,
Pillot, Nîmes, circa 1775–1780.

LOUIS XVI CARVED WALNUT FAUTEUIL EN CABRIOLET, circa 1775–1785.

LOUIS XVI CARVED WALNUT BERGÈRE, circa 1775–1785.

LOUIS XVI CARVED WALNUT CANAPÉ, circa 1775–1785.

LOUIS XVI CARVED WALNUT AND BEECH FAUTEUIL EN CABRIOLET, circa 1780–1790.

LOUIS XVI CARVED WALNUT BERGÈRE, circa 1780–1790.

LOUIS XVI CARVED AND PAINTED DUCHESSE À BATEAU, circa 1780–1790.

Above left:

LOUIS XVI CARVED AND GILDED FAUTEUIL, circa 1785.

Above right:

LOUIS XVI PAINTED CHAISE EN CABRIOLET,
François Lapierre, Lyon, circa 1790.
Courtesy of the Musée Lyonnais des Arts décoratifs.

Left:

LOUIS XVI PAINTED FAUTEUIL EN CABRIOLET, circa 1790.

LOUIS XVI CARVED BEECH MARQUISE,
circa 1780–1790.

LOUIS XVI CARVED, PAINTED AND
PARCEL-GILDED MARQUISE, circa 1790.

LOUIS XVI PAINTED FAUTEUIL
DE BUREAU, circa 1785–1790.

LOUIS XVI PAINTED FAUTEUIL,
circa 1785–1790.

LOUIS XVI WALNUT FAUTEUIL,
François-Noël Geny, Lyon, circa 1790.

LOUIS XVI BEECHWOOD BERGÈRE,
circa 1790.

LOUIS XVI PAINTED FAUTEUIL EN CABRIOLET, circa 1780–1793.

LOUIS XVI PAINTED BERGÈRE EN CABRIOLET, Bordeaux, circa 1780. From a suite of four *fauteuils,* two *bergères,* and a *canapé* made for the *loge Royale du Grand Théâtre*—"in 1780," a date prior to that generally associated with similar designs of Parisian execution. Courtesy of the Musée de Bordeaux.

LOUIS XVI PAINTED BERGÈRE EN CABRIOLET, circa 1780–1793.

LOUIS XVI FRUITWOOD TURQUOISE, circa 1775.
With mark imitating that of Louis Delanois.

LOUIS XVI CARVED AND PAINTED LIT D'ALCOVE, circa 1785.

LOUIS XVI CARVED AND PAINTED LIT DE BOUT
(with coverings and alcove hangings of "toiles des Indes"),
made for the Château Borély, Marseilles, circa 1780.
Courtesy of the Musée d'Archéologie de Marseille.

Above left:

LOUIS XVI TULIPWOOD MARQUETRY PETITE TABLE AMBULANTE, circa 1775–1780.

Above right:

LOUIS XVI TULIPWOOD MARQUETRY TABLE AMBULANTE, circa 1775–1780.

Left:

LOUIS XVI TULIPWOOD MARQUETRY CHIFFONNIÈRE, circa 1775–1780.

LOUIS XVI WALNUT AND MARQUETRY PETITE TABLE À ÉCRIRE, circa 1780–1785. Collection of Monsieur C. Dalbanne, Lyon.

LOUIS XVI TULIPWOOD TABLE DE DAME WITH ÉGLOMISÉ PANELS, circa 1775–1780.

DETAIL OF THE TABLE SHOWN IN THE PRECEDING PLATE. (Above left.)

LOUIS XVI INLAID WALNUT POUDREUSE,
circa 1780–1785.

LOUIS XVI MARQUETRY POUDREUSE,
circa 1780–1785.

LOUIS XVI SYCAMORE MARQUETRY
TABLE AMBULANTE, circa 1780–1785.
Courtesy of French & Company, Inc., New York City.

LOUIS XVI SYCAMORE MARQUETRY
TABLE À COIFFEUSE, circa 1785.

LOUIS XVI TULIPWOOD AND MARQUETRY TABLE À COIFFEUSE, circa 1785.
Courtesy of French & Company, Inc., New York City.

UPPER SURFACES OF THE TABLE SHOWN IN THE PRECEDING PLATE.

LOUIS XVI INLAID FRUITWOOD POUDREUSE, circa 1785.

LOUIS XVI INLAID WALNUT TABLE À JEU,
Claude Gerboud, Lyon, circa 1780–1785.
The panel inlays of palisander and hornbeam.
Courtesy of the Musée Historique de Lyon.

LOUIS XVI MARQUETRY TABLE À GRADIN, circa 1775–1780.

LOUIS XVI TULIPWOOD AND MARQUETRY BONHEUR DU JOUR, circa 1775–1780.
Courtesy of French & Company, Inc., New York City.

LOUIS XVI MARQUETRY BUREAU À CYLINDRE, circa 1775–1780.

LOUIS XVI TULIPWOOD AND MARQUETRY
BUREAU À CYLINDRE, circa 1780–1785.

LOUIS XVI MARQUETRY BUREAU À PENTE, circa 1780–1785.
From Pau, Province of Béarn.

LOUIS XVI INLAID PALISANDER AND TULIPWOOD
BUREAU À CYLINDRE, circa 1780–1790.

LOUIS XVI INLAID AMARANTH AND TULIPWOOD SECRÉTAIRE À RIDEAU, circa 1785–1790.

LOUIS XVI DIRECTOIRE INLAID WALNUT SECRÉTAIRE À RIDEAU, Alsace, circa 1790.

LOUIS XV-XVI CARVED, PAINTED, AND
PARCEL-GILDED CONSOLE, circa 1775.
Courtesy of Monsieur Gaston Bensimon,
New York City.

LOUIS XVI CARVED, PAINTED, AND
PARCEL-GILDED CONSOLE, circa 1775–1780.

LOUIS XVI CARVED AND GILDED CONSOLE, circa 1780–1785.

LOUIS XVI CARVED AND GILDED CONSOLE, circa 1780–1785.

LOUIS XVI CARVED, PAINTED, AND PARCEL-GILDED CONSOLE, circa 1780–1785.

LOUIS XVI CARVED AND GILDED CONSOLE, circa 1785–1790. Courtesy of Frederick P. Victoria, New York City.

LOUIS XV-XVI CHERRYWOOD MARQUETRY
PETITE COMMODE, Grenoble, circa 1775.

LOUIS XVI SYCAMORE MARQUETRY
PETITE COMMODE, Grenoble, circa 1780.

LOUIS XVI CHERRYWOOD MARQUETRY MEUBLE D'ENTREDEUX, circa 1780–1785.

LOUIS XVI MARQUETRY COMMODE, circa 1775–1780. From the Château Borély, Marseille. Courtesy of the Musée d'Archéologie de Marseille.

LOUIS XVI TULIPWOOD, KINGWOOD, AND MARQUETRY COMMODE, circa 1775–1780.

LOUIS XVI TULIPWOOD AND SYCAMORE MARQUETRY COMMODE, circa 1780.
Courtesy of Jacques & Henri Barroux, Paris.

LOUIS XVI SYCAMORE MARQUETRY COMMODE, circa 1780.
Signed BREGUETH, and stamped with the mark of a *Communauté*.

LOUIS XVI SYCAMORE MARQUETRY COMMODE, circa 1780–1785.
With fraudulent mark purporting to be that of François Reizell.

LOUIS XVI MAHOGANY MARQUETRY COMMODE, circa 1785–1790.

LOUIS XVI INLAID MAHOGANY COMMODE, circa 1785–1790.
With mark purporting to be that of François-Barthélemy Crepi.

LOUIS XVI TULIPWOOD MARQUETRY COMMODE, circa 1780–1785.

LOUIS XVI INLAID MAHOGANY AND TULIPWOOD COMMODE, circa 1780–1785.
With mark purporting to be that of Louis Delaître.

LOUIS XVI TULIPWOOD MARQUETRY
PETITE COMMODE, circa 1780–1785.
A type found in Alsatian collections.

LOUIS XVI MARQUETRY COMMODE, circa 1780–1785.

LOUIS XVI MARQUETRY COMMODE, circa 1785.

LOUIS XVI INLAID TULIPWOOD AND MAHOGANY COMMODE, circa 1785.
With a mark purporting to be that of Jacques Bircklé.

LOUIS XVI MARQUETRY COMMODE, circa 1785–1790.

LOUIS XVI INLAID TULIPWOOD COMMODE, circa 1785–1790.

LOUIS XVI INLAID TULIPWOOD SECRÉTAIRE À ABATTANT, circa 1780.

LOUIS XVI INLAID WALNUT SECRÉTAIRE À ABATTANT, Alsace, circa 1780–1785.

LOUIS XVI INLAID TULIPWOOD AND AMARANTH SECRÉTAIRE A ÀBATTANT, circa 1785.

LOUIS XVI INLAID TULIPWOOD SECRÉTAIRE À ABATTANT, circa 1785. Signed F C FONTAINE, and stamped with a *Communauté* mark: JME.

LOUIS XVI MARQUETRY SECRÉTAIRE À ABATTANT, circa 1785.

LOUIS XVI AMARANTH AND TULIPWOOD MARQUETRY SECRÉTAIRE À ABATTANT, circa 1785. Stamped with the initials E H B.

LOUIS XVI MARQUETRY SECRÉTAIRE
À ABATTANT, circa 1785.

OUIS XVI INLAID TULIPWOOD SECRÉTAIRE À ABATTANT, circa 1785.

LOUIS XVI CARVED AND GILDED WALL MIRROR, circa 1775–1780.

LOUIS XVI CARVED AND GILDED WALL MIRROR, circa 1785.

LOUIS XVI CARVED AND GILDED WALL MIRROR, circa 1785.

LOUIS XVI CARVED AND GILDED WALL MIRROR, circa 1785–1790.

LOUIS XVI CARVED AND GILDED WALL MIRROR, circa 1785.

LOUIS XVI CARVED AND GILDED WALL MIRROR, circa 1785.

LOUIS XVI CARVED AND GILDED WALL MIRROR, Marseille, circa 1785.

LOUIS XVI CARVED AND GILDED WALL MIRROR, Marseille, circa 1785.

LOUIS XVI CARVED, PAINTED AND PARCEL-GILDED BAROMÈTRE À CADRAN, circa 1775–1785.

LOUIS XVI CARVED AND GILDED BAROMÈTRE À CADRAN, circa 1785.

DIRECTOIRE-CONSULATE CARVED WALNUT AND HORNBEAM CHAISE, circa 1795–1801.
Nicolas Parmantier, Lyon.
Courtesy of the Musée Historique de Lyon.

DIRECTOIRE BEECHWOOD FAUTEUIL À DOSSIER RENVERSÉ, circa 1795–1799.

DIRECTOIRE-CONSULATE FAUTEUIL À DOSSIER RENVERSÉ, circa 1795–1801.
Nicolas Parmantier, Lyon.
Courtesy of the Musée Historique de Lyon.

CONSULATE CARVED WALNUT CHAISE, circa 1799–1804.
Similar to a model made by Antoine Parmantier of Lyon, but with less refined molding work.

DIRECTOIRE WALNUT CANAPÉ, circa 1795–1799.

DIRECTOIRE PAINTED CANAPÉ, circa 1795–1799.

DIRECTOIRE MAHOGANY GUÉRIDON À PUPITRE, circa 1795–1799.

DIRECTOIRE MAHOGANY TABLE À RIDEAU, circa 1795–1799.

DIRECTOIRE MAHOGANY TABLE À TRICTRAC, circa 1795–1799.

DIRECTOIRE MAHOGANY TABLE À DÉJEUNER, circa 1795–1799.

DIRECTOIRE MAHOGANY DESSERTE, circa 1795–1799.

DIRECTOIRE MAHOGANY DESSERTE, circa 1795–1799.
Courtesy of J. J. Wolff Antiques Ltd., New York City.

DIRECTOIRE MAHOGANY COMMODE, circa 1795–1799.

Above:
DIRECTOIRE MAHOGANY COMMODE, circa 1795–1799.

Right:
DIRECTOIRE MAHOGANY SECRÉTAIRE À ABATTANT, circa 1795–1799.

METROPOLITAN, SUBURBAN, AND RURAL FURNITURE OF THE FRENCH PROVINCES AND OTHER EUROPEAN COUNTRIES

(Principally representative of *Menuiserie* as executed in leading furniture centres)

CARVED AND PAINTED PRIE-DIEU, circa 1735–1755.

CARVED BEECHWOOD CHAISE RUSTIQUE,
Provence, circa 1740–1750.

CARVED BEECHWOOD CHAISE
PERCÉE, circa 1750–1770.

CARVED BEECHWOOD FAUTEUIL RUSTIQUE,
Provence or Dauphiné, circa 1740–1760.

CARVED ASH BERGÈRE À OREILLES, circa 1740–1760.

CARVED BEECHWOOD BERGÈRE À OREILLES, circa 1740–1760.

CARVED WALNUT CANAPÉ À OREILLES, circa 1745–1765.
Courtesy of the Musée et Bibliothèque Calvet, Avignon.

CARVED WALNUT TABLE-CONSOLE, Provence, circa 1740–1760.

CARVED WALNUT BUREAU À PENTE, Provence, circa 1740–1760.

CARVED WALNUT BUREAU À PENTE, circa 1745–1765.
Courtesy of the Musée et Bibliothèque Calvet, Avignon.

FRUITWOOD BUREAU À PENTE, circa 1760–1780. Of a design duplicated in both northern and southern provinces.

FRUITWOOD AND BEECHWOOD BUREAU PLAT, circa 1740–1760.

FRUITWOOD BUREAU PLAT, circa 1755–1770. The general design also produced in veneered and inlaid work of numerous furniture centres.

CARVED WALNUT TABLE-CONSOLE, Provence, 18th Century (1735+).

CARVED WALNUT TABLE-CONSOLE, Provence, 18th Century (1750+).

WALNUT COMMODE OR CASSETTONE, Provence, 18th Century (1735+).

WALNUT COMMODE, Provence, 18th Century (1735+).

WALNUT COMMODE,
18th Century (1745+).
With recessed panel moldings, a treatment favored in various French provinces and in Piedmonte.

WALNUT COMMODE,
18th Century (1745+).
With use of Italian poplar as a secondary material, an additional indication of southern workmanship; the piece reduced in depth.

CARVED WALNUT PETITE COMMODE EN CONSOLE,
circa 1745–1755. Style of Arles.

CARVED AND INLAID WALNUT COMMODE GALBÉE,
circa 1745–1755.

Top:

CARVED AND TURNED WALNUT PANETIÈRE, Provence, 18th Century (1745+).

Bottom:

CARVED WALNUT COMMODE, Provence, circa 1750–1760. Style of Arles.

CARVED WALNUT COMMODE GALBÉE, Arles, circa 1750–1760.
A handsome metropolitan example, finer in quality of form and ornamentation than many of the solidly constructed case pieces produced in more northerly cities of the Continent, or in the British provinces of colonial America.

WALNUT COMMODE À PIEDS,
circa 1760–1770.

CARVED WALNUT COMMODE À PIEDS, Provence,
circa 1760–1770. Style of Arles.

CARVED WALNUT BUFFET À DEUX PORTES, 18th Century (1720+).
Courtesy of the Musée Lyonnais des Arts décoratifs.

CARVED OAK BUFFET BAS,
18th Century (1770+).

MAHOGANY SECRÉTAIRE-BIBLIOTHÈQUE, 18th Century (1760+).
Courtesy of the Musée des Arts décoratifs, Paris.

OAK BUFFET-VAISSELIER, Bretagne, 18th Century (1735+).

CARVED OAK AND FRUITWOOD ARMOIRE, 18th Century (1735+).

CARVED OAK ARMOIRE, Île de France, circa 1735.
Courtesy of the Musée des Arts décoratifs, Paris.

CARVED OAK ARMOIRE DE SACRISTIE, Aix, circa 1740–1755.
Courtesy of the Musée des Arts décoratifs, Paris.

CARVED OAK ARMOIRE, Normandie, circa 1770–1785.
Courtesy of the Musea van Oudhedan, Antwerp.

CARVED AND GILDED WALL MIRROR, circa 1750–1770.

CARVED AND GILDED WALL MIRROR, circa 1760–1775.

PAINTED AND DECORATED FANTEUIL "BONNE FEMME," 18th Century (1760+).

CARVED AND TURNED FRUITWOOD FAUTEUIL "BONNE FEMME," Provence or Comtat, circa 1780–1800.

CARVED WALNUT FAUTEUIL DE BUREAU, circa 1780–1800.

CARVED WALNUT BERGÈRE, circa 1780–1800.

FRUITWOOD CHIFFONNIÈRE,
circa 1775–1800.

INLAID WALNUT TABLE DE CHEVET,
circa 1780–1800.

WALNUT RAFRAÎCHISSOIR,
circa 1775–1800.

INLAID CHERRYWOOD CHIFFONNIÈRE,
circa 1775–1800.

INLAID CHERRYWOOD CHIFFONNIÈRE,
circa 1775–1800.

MAHOGANY RAFRAÎCHISSOIR, Paris, circa 1775.
Attributed to Joseph Gengenbach, known as
Canabas (r. m. 1766).
Courtesy of the Musée Nissim de Camondo, Paris.

WALNUT RAFRAÎCHISSOIR,
circa 1775–1800.

FRUITWOOD RAFRAÎCHISSOIR,
circa 1775–1800.

WALNUT TABLE-LISEUSE, circa 1775–1800.

WALNUT TABLE DE MILIEU, circa 1785–1800.

CARVED WALNUT CONSOLE, Provence, circa 1780–1800.

CARVED AND GILDED CONSOLE,
Provence, circa 1780–1800.
Courtesy of French & Company, Inc.,
New York City.

CHERRYWOOD PETITE COMMODE,
Grenoble, circa 1775–1785.

WALNUT COMMODE À PIEDS,
circa 1775–1785. Style of Grenoble.

WALNUT COMMODE, circa 1790–1800.

WALNUT COMMODE, circa 1795–1805.

CARVED OAK ARMOIRE, circa 1775–1800.

CARVED MAHOGANY ARMOIRE,
Bordeau, circa 1780–1790.
Courtesy of the Musée des Arts décoratifs, Paris.

CARVED WALNUT BUFFET À DEUX CORPS, circa 1770–1820.

CARVED AND GILDED WALL MIRROR,
circa 1780–1800.

CARVED AND GILDED WALL MIRROR,
Provence, circa 1780–1800.

GILDED WALL MIRROR WITH GESSO RELIEF ORNAMENT. Correctly advertised as of the late nineteenth century, but arbitarily illustrated as an eighteenth-century example in an American publication on "French provincial" furniture. In their relief ornament, French craftsmen of the eighteenth century never employed gesso on a smooth, uncarved wood ground.

CARVED AND INLAID FRUITWOOD AND WALNUT ARMOIRE, dated 1838.
Style of Rennes.

LOUIS XV FAUTEUIL EN CABRIOLET, Swiss, 18th Century.
From the Maison Pourtales, Neuchâtel.
Courtesy of the Musée Historique Bernois.

LOUIS XVI CHAISE EN CABRIOLET, Berne, circa 1775.
Courtesy of the Musée Historique Bernois.

LOUIS XVI PAINTED AND PARCEL-GILDED CHAISE, EN CABRIOLET.
Flemish, Late 18th Century. Copyright A C L Bruxelles.

LOUIS XVI CARVED AND GILDED FAUTEUIL, Brussels, circa 1785. Copyright A C L Bruxelles.

LATE LOUIS XVI CARVED AND GILDED CHAISE CANNÉ, Brussels, circa 1790. Copyright A C L Bruxelles.

LOUIS XVI CARVED AND GILDED TABOURET, Ghent, circa 1785. Copyright A C L Bruxelles.

LOUIS XVI CARVED, PAINTED, AND GILDED FAUTEUIL EN CABRIOLET, Brussels, circa 1785. Copyright A C L Bruxelles.

LOUIS XVI CARVED, PAINTED, AND GILDED CANAPÉ À JOUE, Brussels, circa 1785. Copyright A C L Bruxelles.

LOUIS XVI ACAJOU TABLE À JEU, MOUNTED IN BRONZE DORÉ, Flemish (attributed to Brussels), circa 1790. Copyright A C L Bruxelles.

LOUIS XV CARVED AND GILDED CONSOLE, Antwerp, circa 1750. Copyright A C L Bruxelles.

LOUIS XV CARVED AND GILDED CONSOLE, Liége, circa 1750. Copyright A C L Bruxelles.

LOUIS XV CARVED AND GILDED CONSOLE, Liége (Huy), circa 1750.
Copyright A C L Bruxelles.

LOUIS XV CARVED OAK TABLE-CONSOLE, Liége, circa 1750.
Copyright A C L Bruxelles.

LOUIS XV CARVED OAK COMMODE, Liége, circa 1750.
Courtesy of the Musea Van Oudheden, Antwerp.

LOUIS XV INLAID BURLWOOD COMMODE, MOUNTED IN BRONZE DORÉ,
Namur, circa 1750–1760. Copyright A C L Bruxelles.

LOUIS XV COMMODE À PIEDS, MOUNTED IN BRONZE DORÉ, Mathäus Funk, Berne, circa 1760. With customary plateau of Grindelwald marble.
Courtesy of the Musée Historique Bernois.

LOUIS XVI CARVED OAK COMMODE, Flemish, circa 1780.
Copyright A C L Bruxelles.

LOUIS XVI CARVED OAK COMMODE-SECRÉTAIRE, Liége, circa 1770.
Copyright A C L Bruxelles.

LOUIS XVI MARQUETRY COMMODE, MOUNTED IN BRONZE DORÉ, Swedish, circa 1785. Courtesy of the Nordiska Museet, Stockholm.

LOUIS XVI MARQUETRY COMMODE, Swedish, circa 1790. Published as "French Provincial"; actually produced in the Swedish capital, probably by the master cabinetmaker Gustaf Foltiern (or Foltjern).

LOUIS XV LAVISHLY INLAID AND FITTED BUREAU À PENTE,
Abraham and David Roentgen, Neuwied, circa 1765.
Courtesy of the Rijksmuseum, Amsterdam.

LOUIS XV CARVED OAK AND PARQUETRY COMMODE SECRÉTAIRE, Liége, circa 1750.
Copyright A C L Bruxelles.

LOUIS XV-XVI CARVED OAK BUREAU À CYLINDRE, Antwerp, circa 1765.
Courtesy of the Musea Van Oudheden, Antwerp.

Above:

LOUIS XVI BUREAU À PENTE, Flemish (Limbourg), circa 1785. Copyright A C L Bruxelles.

Right:

LOUIS XVI CARVED OAK BUREAU-BIBLIOTHÈQUE, Liége, circa 1785. Copyright A C L Bruxelles.

LOUIS XV CARVED AND INLAID BUFFET À DEUX CORPS,
Ardennes, 18th Century. Copyright A C L Bruxelles.

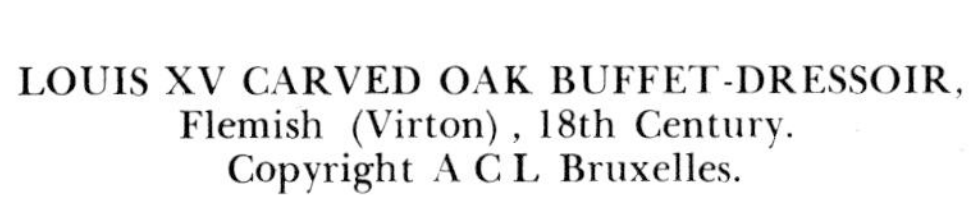

LOUIS XV CARVED OAK BUFFET-DRESSOIR,
Flemish (Virton), 18th Century.
Copyright A C L Bruxelles.

LOUIS XV INLAID OAK ARMOIRE OR LINGÈRE, Ardennes, 18th Century.
Copyright A C L Bruxelles.

LOUIS XV CARVED OAK BUFFET, Liége, circa 1750.
Courtesy of the Musée des Arts décoratifs, Paris.

LOUIS XV CARVED OAK GRANDE ARMOIRE, Liége, circa 1750. Copyright A C L Bruxelles.

LOUIS XV CARVED OAK ARMOIRE VITRÉ, 18th Century. Style of Normandie; believed to have actually been produced in Liége. Copyright A C L Bruxelles.

Right:

LOUIS XV CARVED AND GILDED ÉCRAN, Flemish (attributed to Ghent), circa 1750. Copyright A C L Bruxelles.

Below right:

LOUIS XV CARVED AND GILDED WALL MIRROR, Schleswig-Holstein, circa 1760–1770. Courtesy of the Schleswig-Holsteinisches Landesmuseum, Kiel.

Below left:

LOUIS XV CARVED AND PAINTED OAK ENCADREMENT, WITH OIL PAINTING, Liégè, circa 1760. Copyright A C L Bruxelles.

LOUIS XVI CARVED OAK HORLOGE, Liége (Verviers), circa 1785.

LOUIS XV CARVED OAK HORLOGE, Liége (Verviers), circa 1760. Copyright A C L Bruxelles.

BIBLIOGRAPHY

Algoud, H. *Le Mobilier Provençal.* Paris: n.d.

Avril, Paul. *L'Ameublement Parisian.* Paris: 1929.

Banéat, P. *Le Mobilier Breton.* Paris: n.d.

Champier, V. *Le Mobilier Flamand.* Paris: n.d.

Clouzot, Henri. *Les Meubles du XVIIIe Siècle.* Paris: 1922.

D'Agnel, G. Arnaud. *Le Meuble (Ameublement Provençal & Camtadin).* Marseille: 1929.

De Champeaux, Alfred. *Le Meuble.* Paris: n.d.

Delafosse, Jean Charles. *L'Oeuvre de.* Paris: 1772.

Delaye, Edmond. *Quelques Menuisiers en Sièges de Lyon.* Lyon: 1936.

De Ricci, Seymour. *Le Style Louis XVI, Mobilier et Décoration.* Paris: 1913.

______. *Louis XIV and Régence Furniture and Decoration.* New York: 1929.

De Salverte, Comte François. *Le Meuble Français d'après les Ornemanistes.* Paris: 1930.

Dilke, Lady Emilia F. S. *French Furniture and Decoration in the XVIIIth Century.* London: 1901.

Dumonthier, Ernest. *The Louis XVI Furniture.* Paris: 1922.

Feuldner, Adolf. *Kunstgeschichte des Möbels.* Berlin: 1927.

Fischer, Ernst. *Svenska Mobler i Bild.* Stockholm: 1931.

Fouquier, Marcel. *Les Belles Adventures d'un Marteau d'Ivoire.* Paris: 1948.

______. *Le Mobilier des Vielles Provinces Françaises.* Paris: n.d.

Gauthier, J. *Le Mobilier Auvergnat.* Paris: n.d.

______. *Le Mobilier Vendéen.* Paris: n.d.

______. *La Connaissance des Meubles Régionaux Français.* Paris: 1852.

Gélis, P. *Le Mobilier Alsacien.* Paris: n.d.

Giroud & Delaye. *Les Hache, Ébénistes de Grenoble.* Grenoble: n.d.

Guerinet, A. (ed.). *L'Art Ancien du Mobilier au Pays de Liége.* Paris: n.d.

Henriot, Gabriel. *Les Beaux meubles des Collections Privées.* Paris: n.d.

Huth, Hans. *Abraham und David Roentgen.* Berlin: 1928.

Janneau, Guillaume. *Le Meuble Léger en France.* Paris: 1952.

______. *Le Siège en France.* Paris: 1948.

______. *Les Commodes.* Paris: n.d.

———. *Les Grands Meubles.* Paris: n.d.
———. *Les Petits Meubles.* Paris: n.d.
———. *Les Sièges.* Paris: n.d.
———. *Lits de Repos & Lits.* Paris: n.d.
Lagerquist, Marshall. *Rokokomöbler.* Stockholm: 1949.
Laking, Guy Francis. *The Furniture of Windsor Castle.* London: n.d.
Le Clerc, L. *Le Mobilier Normand.* Paris: n.d.
Lee, Morton. *An Exhibition: The Royal Cabinet Makers of France.* London: 1951.
Lemaire, Kan. R. *Beknopte Geschiedenis van de Meubelkunst.* Antwerp: 1945.
Lucotte, J.-R. *Menuisier en Meubles.* Paris: n.d. (c. 1769).
Maumené, Albert. *Les Beaux Meubles Régionaux des Provinces de France.* Paris: 1952.
Molinier, Émile. *Les Meubles.* Paris: n.d.
Mottheau, Jacques. *Meubles Usuels, Directoire-Empire.* Paris: n.d.
———. *Meubles Usuels, Louis XVI.* Paris: n.d.
———. *Meubles Usuels, Régence-Louis XV.* Paris: n.d.
Roche, Denis. *Le Mobilier Français en Russie.* Paris: n.d.
Roubo, A.-J. *L'Art du Menuisier en Meubles.* Paris: 1772.
Sadoul, C. *Le Mobilier Lorrain.* Paris: n.d.
Schoenen, Paul. *Aachener und Lutticher Möbel des 18. Jahrhunderts.* Berlin: 1942.
Smith, H. Clifford. *Buckingham Palace.* London: 1930.
Strange, Thomas Arthur. *French Interiors, Furniture, Decoration, Woodwork & Allied Arts.* London: n.d.
Tardieu, Suzanne. *Meubles Régionaux Datés.* Paris: 1950.
Terme, M. G. *L'Art Ancien au Pays de Liége.* Liége: n.d.
Verlet, Pierre. *Le Mobilier Royal Français.* Paris: 1945.
Wallin, Sigurd. *Nordiska Museets Möbler fran Svenska Herremanshem.* Stockholm: 1931.